JESUS, THE KING OF KINGS

LEELA A. A. EAPEN

Jesus, the King of Kings

Trilogy Christian Publishers A Wholly Owned Subsidiary of Trinity Broadcasting Network

2442 Michelle Drive Tustin, CA 92780

Copyright © 2024 by Leela A. A. Eapen

Unless otherwise indicated, Scripture quotations are taken from The Holy Bible, New International Version Copyright © 1973, 1978, 1984 by International Bible Society. Used by permission of Zondervan. All rights reserved.

Scripture quotations identified as AMP are taken from The Amplified Bible, Old Testament copyright © 1965, 1987 by the Zondervan Corporation. The Amplified New Testament copyright © 1958, 1987 by the Lockman Foundation. Used by permission.

Scripture quotations identified as NCV are taken from "The Holy Bible, New Century Verson®," copyright © 2005 by Thomas Nelson, Inc. Used by permission.

Scripture quotations identified as NKJV are taken from New King James Version®, copyright © 1982 by Thomas Nelson, Inc. Used by permission. All rights reserved

No part of this book may be reproduced, stored in a retrieval system, or transmitted by any means without written permission from the author. All rights reserved. Printed in the USA.

Rights Department, 2442 Michelle Drive, Tustin, CA 92780.

Trilogy Christian Publishing/TBN and colophon are trademarks of Trinity Broadcasting Network.

For information about special discounts for bulk purchases, please contact Trilogy Christian Publishing.

Trilogy Disclaimer: The views and content expressed in this book are those of the author and may not necessarily reflect the views and doctrine of Trilogy Christian Publishing or the Trinity Broadcasting Network.

10 9 8 7 6 5 4 3 2 1

Library of Congress Cataloging-in-Publication Data is available.

ISBN: 979-8-89041-264-5

E-ISBN: 979-8-89041-265-2

This book is dedicated to the Holy Trinity, for the message from the beginning to the end is from God the Father; the book is about His Son Jesus Christ, the King of all kings, and the Holy Spirit guided me throughout the writing process. Therefore, all the glory, honor, and praise belong to the Triune God.

ACKNOWLEDGMENTS

My heartfelt thanks go to the following people:

Carolyn Weeks May, my writer: Even with all of your disabilities, only one thing was in your heart—"serve the Lord"—and you did it. Without you, this book wouldn't have taken shape.

Simon, my beloved husband: You helped me find a writer, and you let me go to her home practically every day, where I spent hours and hours of my life for the past four years.

Maureen, my loving daughter: I totally depended on your computer skills and your marvelous intellect, which helped me to initiate the original manuscript. And you never hesitated but gladly helped me continuously whenever I needed it.

Simon, my loving son: You are like the one who is depicted in Proverbs 1:8–9. You have always listened with great attentiveness to the teachings and instructions of your parents and also your sister. You give me great peace and happiness. I also thank Teena, your wife, who is now on board and has helped me greatly with the computer work.

Reverend Father John Thomas: Your humility, love, and compassion toward our family and your prayers are highly appreciated.

I thank all the biblical scholars who put their minds and hearts together and, guided by the Holy Spirit, worked so hard to make these study Bibles available to the public (especially to people like me) and glorify God Almighty.

I thank all my teachers at the New York School of the Bible and its faculty, for without these special people, I would still be struggling to know what the Bible is really all about.

Dr. Annie Mundeke, PhD, one of the teachers at the New York School of the Bible: You believed in the vision and helped me with my original outline of this book. Later on, God began giving me many additions.

My prayer warriors: Norma the prophetess, Bill, Huey, Daniel, Roger, Carolyn, Pastor Lee; all my sisters on the daily teleconference prayer-line: Lemma, Christine, Hedy, and Cassandra; Liz and her Bible study group; my church; Rev. Dr. Mathew Koshy and the whole congregation; my beloved family, and many others.

Reverle: After Carolyn left for Texas to be with her husband, and when I thought the time had come for publishing the book, you came to my aid. Selflessly, you helped me with the computer work on various occasions.

Lori Kunde of BookFuel, you're a woman of God, and I thank God for bringing you into my life. You and your team's earnest work toward this book is unremarkable.

I thank CreateSpace for granting my request for a Christian editor who is faithful and knowledgeable in the Word.

I thank great editors like Miranda and Nichole from the bottom of my heart for not only editing but also for your teachings, advice, guidance, and gracious comments.

I thank Norma, my prophetess, for in my anguish, God once again sent you all the way from New Jersey to Georgia for a third round of editing, and you are an awesome editor! Even after leaving, you have continued to help me as the time permitted.

BookFuel Publishing: I thank you again for your kindness and gentleness in teaching, correcting, and guiding me through the final round of editing.

My heartfelt thanks and blessings to TBN/Trilogy Publishing House for accepting the new authors', especially mine, God-inspired books. I'm truly humbled by your gracious comments made on the manuscript; none is my ability; all is from above. So, I give all the glory and honor to Him and Him alone! The Lord heard my

ACKNOWLEDGMENTS

years of crying and prayers and opened the door for me to publish His book through a reputable publishing house. Ms. Stacy Baker, I thank you from the bottom of my heart for your quick response to my application and your perseverance, which helped me accomplish the long-waited desire of my heart, and that is, to publish the Lord's book through a reputable publishing house. I pray, may the Lord bless hundred-fold the TBN, Trilogy Publishing, Stacy, and all those who are involved in this project in glorifying His name.

TABLE OF CONTENTS

Acknowledgments 5

Introduction 11

Chapter 1: The Vision 15

Chapter 2: The Meaning of the Vision 17

Chapter 3: Prophecies about the Coming of Jesus (the Messiah) and Their Fulfillment 19

Chapter 4: My Experience as a Christian 35

Chapter 5: What Was the Purpose of His Coming? 47

Chapter 6: The Light in the Midst of the Darkness 81

Chapter 7: The Fulfillment of the Prophecies Regarding Jesus' Suffering 89

Chapter 8: The Crucifixion 117

Chapter 9: The Resurrection 131

Chapter 10: Who Am I, Oh Lord, That You Have Brought Me So Far? 141

Chapter 11: The Great Day of the Lord 159

Chapter 12: From the Beginning to the End? 183

Chapter 13: God's Amazing Mercy 199

Chapter 14: God's Amazing Grace 211

Addendum 223

About the Author 227

INTRODUCTION

Although there are nearly two and a half billion Christians in the world, I often wonder how many are acquainted with the written Word of God! I'm in awe to know there are people afraid of opening their Bible for they know not what to look for or where to begin. "I pray, this book will guide and encourage you not only to read but study them." Because the Bible will give you knowledge and understanding as to who God is and help you grow your faith and relationship with Him through His Son Jesus.

Like many, I'm just a layperson who has struggled to know what the Holy Bible is all about. I pray that this book will benefit those who call themselves Christians yet haven't had a chance to study the Word of God or don't have an intimate relationship with Jesus, like me in my past life; all the nonbelievers all over the world, who have never received Jesus as their Lord and Savior; those who turned away from the Christian faith. May this book be a blessing to you from generation to generation. My humble desire is to encourage and motivate to study the Bible and be obedient children of God: Jesus said, "If you love me, you will obey what I command" (John 14:15). How will we know what His commandments are if we don't learn or know His teachings?

I knew I was not worthy to write this book, for I'm poor in language and immature in Scriptures. This assignment should have been given to a biblical scholar, not me—and yet, with all my weaknesses, the Lord still chose and used me to accomplish His purpose and His plan. My deepest desire was to obey God's command and to be a productive servant of my Lord with the talent He had given me.

The Creator of heaven and Earth, the living God, keeps no secret from us. He reveals His plans ahead of time (Isaiah 46:9–10;

Amos 3:7). This He does for our spiritual readiness and to prepare us for future events. Surely, the Lord will never fail to accomplish His plans (Isaiah 55:11). We notice in the Old Testament, from the book of Genesis through Malachi, God the Father's plans, the promises He had made, and the purpose for sending His Son into this world. The proof of their fulfillment had been recorded in the New Testament, especially in the Gospels of Matthew, Mark, Luke, and John. We are now anxiously waiting for another promise God has made—"the return of Jesus Christ." Are you ready for this great event?

This book contains some of the prophecies and their fulfillments about Jesus' birth, His teachings, suffering, crucifixion, resurrection, and the ascension to His heavenly Father. Also included are some of the prophecies about His second advent and how to prepare ourselves as we wait.

I truly believe He never changes, "Jesus Christ is the same yesterday and today and forever" (Hebrews 13:8). As He guided those unschooled fishermen to write His message two thousand years ago that He may be glorified, so has the Lord guided me to write this book, to glorify His name! He will do the same or even abundantly more if you are simply willing. God is not looking for an Oxford graduate but a humble and obedient heart.

By spending more time studying the Holy Bible, you will become courageous, not fearful. It will increase your spiritual strength because God's Spirit will dwell in you (John 14:17c). His words are mighty in power: they direct and guide our thoughts, minds, and hearts to the right path, so we sin less, and thus make us righteous or godly. He leads us into the "highway to heaven," where we will spend eternity with the Lord.

Keep your Holy Bible by your side as you read this book since there will be a need to open and read whenever you notice references and, "please read for your understanding." The more you flip

INTRODUCTION

through the pages, the more you will become acquainted with the names of the books in the Bible and their location. This practice will give you more knowledge, comfort, and excitement in studying the Scriptures.

I pray that the Lord will give you visions as God foretold through prophet Joel (Joel 2:28–29), transform your hearts, guide you along your journey, and accomplish His set purpose for you in this world.

Jesus loves you,

May the Lord God bless the reader.

CHAPTER 1:

THE VISION

Although the vision lasted only a brief moment, little did I know the impact that it would have on my life for many years to come.

For the past couple of years, I'd had a compelling desire to write a book on how the Lord took Saul (Paul), the persecutor of Christians, and turned him into a pillar of the early church.

During this same period of time, I had considered writing a book on the seven churches in Asia Minor from the book of Revelation. The motive for my writing has always been to glorify the Lord and to bless the reader, so it seemed that I was continuously asking God, "Which way should I go, Lord?"

On Saturday evening, April 9, 2005, I wasn't feeling quite up to par, and rather than taking a chance on disturbing my husband's sleep, I made a decision to spend the night on the daybed in my son Simon's room. It turned out to be so comfortable I slept peacefully all night. At approximately 11 a.m., I glanced across the room at the clock radio Simon kept on his computer desk; I realized I had missed church. Suddenly, I began thinking about what would usually be happening on Sunday mornings at around this time. I started visualizing the priest consecrating the bread and wine in preparation for Communion.

I immediately sat up on the side of the bed, made the sign of the cross, and said a little silent prayer in the quietness of my mind. Since I was still feeling tired and weak, I quickly fell back into a deep sleep. I was awakened in less than an hour by a voice clearly telling me, "Write this down!" Then I saw a vivid vision of a hand holding a white piece of chalk, and it was writing and underlining "Jesus, the King of kings" on the cast-iron bedboard. The whole vision took place faster than the speed of lightning.

As I became more awake, I asked the Lord, "Father, what shall I do with this?" He then implanted the following Bible verses in my heart, "*In the beginning was the Word, and the Word was with God, and the Word was God ...The Word became flesh*" (John 1:1, 14a) (emphasis added by the author). I quickly stood to my feet and started writing down everything the Lord was giving me.

I looked at the clock and noticed that it was 11:50 a.m. As I continuously prayed and asked the Lord to lead me step by step, I truly had no idea of how many steps lay ahead of me. God the Father took me to the book of Genesis, the creation, then chapter three, verse fifteen. From there, He graciously guided me to the books of Deuteronomy, 2 Samuel, many of the prophets and their prophecies, the Gospels, some epistles, and the book of Revelation. It took me over five hours to compile all the information He had to give me. Only by His grace did I have the strength to stand for that entire time, which I chose to do in reverence for my Father and His Word. I did take a couple of very short breaks but immediately returned to work in continuous prayer. Amazingly, I no longer felt ill; in fact, I seemed to have an abundance of energy, happiness, and joy as I knelt and bowed down to praise and thank the Lord. The time was 5:39 p.m.

CHAPTER 2:

THE MEANING OF THE VISION

I spent many hours writing down the information the Lord had given me for this book, and yet, I still didn't have a clue as to how to format or organize all the material that I had compiled. A few days later, I called the person who was the leader of the women's groups in the Indian Orthodox Churches in the United States, Liziamma Kuruvilla, and I proceeded to tell her, "I know that in the past, it's been a common practice to have the priest conduct the women's Bible studies up at the church, but for now, I'll be conducting the current class in my home."

She asked me, "What is the subject of your class going to be?"

I replied, "Jesus, the King of kings."

The leader then said, "That's a very big subject. How can you teach it in a day?"

I quickly answered her it would be no problem, for I could divide the teaching into three parts: prophecy about Jesus' birth, prophecy about His missionary work, death, and resurrection, and prophecy about His second coming. The group leader was extremely happy upon hearing my intentions for teaching the Bible study, and we ended the conversation on a positive note.

Upon completing the call, I suddenly realized that not a single statement or answer to this question came from my own knowledge, mind, or heart, but it was God Himself who put His thoughts in my mind and His words in my mouth. I acknowledge more every day that I could not possibly have come up with such big thoughts—in fact, I would never be able to! *It was His way of showing me what to write about Him and how He wanted it written.*

The last thing I did in this sequence of events was to contact the parish priest and tell him all about our plan for the Bible study that would be meeting in my home. I invited Father John Thomas to come to bless us and pray for us. I placed one stipulation on his invitation to participate: he had to leave after his prayer because I would be conducting the class. Father agreed to abide by the condition placed on his invitation, and he lived up to his agreement.

The first class was held on April 30, 2005, from 10 a.m. until 2 p.m., and although it was a small group of nine ladies, they all talked about how much they enjoyed it and commented that we should have more in-home Bible classes. Truly, the Lord blessed us to continue the Bible classes, although not in my own house, but we chose to conduct it in someone else's home, who was disabled to travel, but her heart desired it. Some of the ladies enjoyed the class so much that they drove for an hour just to be in attendance.

I remember one particular occasion when one of the ladies from the class called me and told me that she would really like to learn more about the Bible. It has always been my desire to share with others the knowledge I worked so hard to gain at the Bible school. Because I could see her deep, sincere hunger for the Word of God, we set a date to meet in the church basement for a one-on-one Bible study. This young woman was so excited about her opportunity to learn the Scriptures, verse by verse, that we became totally immersed in the words of God, and before we knew it, five hours had flown by without us even realizing it.

CHAPTER 3:

PROPHECIES ABOUT THE COMING OF JESUS (THE MESSIAH) AND THEIR FULFILLMENT

It seems God always reveals His plans to His people way ahead of time, for example, "Surely the Sovereign LORD does nothing without revealing his plan to his servants the prophets" (Amos 3:7). So, the people could be ready when the event takes place.

Over fourteen hundred years prior to the birth of King Jesus, God declared to Moses,

> *I will raise up for them a prophet like you from among their brothers [amongst the Israelites]; I will put my words in his mouth, and he will tell them everything I command him. If anyone does not listen to my words that the prophet speaks in my name, I myself will call him to account.*
>
> **Deuteronomy 18:18–19**
> **(Emphasis added by the author)**

As we continue to study the Old Testament, we can see that the Lord spoke to many prophets at various times, telling them that He would be sending His Son through the royal line of His servant David. Some religions believe that Jesus was simply a prophet, but I pray that the Lord will make it perfectly clear to you that He was the Son of the Most High, and He Himself was God, the Creator of all things (John 1:1–3, 14). Since God was sending His own Son, He expected that the people would accept His messages just as He intended. Those who chose to reject them could expect the most severe punishment.

We notice in the Old Testament times, God constantly disciplined those who disobeyed His command. The prophet Samuel spoke to Saul, the first king of Israel, when he was severely punished due to his disobedience of God's command, "But now your kingdom will not endure; the LORD has sought out a man after his own heart and appointed him leader of his people, because you have not kept the LORD's command" (1 Samuel 13:13–14). Of course, this type of worldly discipline is nothing in comparison to the unimaginable suffering waiting in eternal punishment. It was at this time that God chose to remove Saul from his position as king of the Israelites and instead make David the king.

Although David was just a shepherd boy, God saw his heart and chose him to be the ruler over His people. After many years of battle with his enemies, David was relaxing in his luxurious palace, finished with the expensive acacia wood (which had been donated by his royal friends). In his humility, he felt it was his responsibility to build a temple for the Lord. So, he expressed his concern to the prophet Nathan that the ark of the covenant existed in a tent and traveled from place to place while he was living in such luxury, and he wanted to build a permanent dwelling for the ark of the Lord. Without consulting God, Nathan told David that the Lord had always been good to him and that he should carry out whatever plans he had made. Soon, they would find out what a

PROPHECIES ABOUT THE COMING OF JESUS

huge blessing and mighty plan the Lord had stored up for the king.

That very same night, God appeared to Nathan and declared to him the covenant He was making with His servant David. This took place about four hundred years after God made His promise to Moses,

> *When your days are over and you rest with your fathers, I will raise up your offspring to succeed you ... and I will establish the throne of his kingdom forever. I will be his father, and he will be my son. ...Your house and your kingdom will endure forever before me; your throne will be established forever.*
>
> **2 Samuel 7:12a–c, 13b–14a, 16
> (Emphasis added by the author)**

This was the promise God made to David that, years after his death, the Son of God (Jesus) would be born from David's family lineage, and His kingdom would be established forever. What was so important about God bringing His Son into the world through the lineage of David? I believe it's because David had a heart like God (1 Samuel 13:14). He was not only a shepherd but a warrior, a king, and a poet who wrote about seventy-five Psalms, and he also was a prophet. He prophesied many words regarding Jesus Christ. The genealogy of Jesus Christ is recorded in Matthew 1:1–17 and Luke 3:23–38. Please read for your understanding.

Somewhere between 740 and 681 BC, hundreds of years after the death of David and his father Jesse, God revealed to Isaiah, "A shoot will come up from the stump of Jesse; from his roots a Branch will bear fruit" (Isaiah 11:1). Here when God spoke of a shoot or a Branch, He was referring to His own Son, a descendant of David, Jesus Christ (the Messiah).

God spoke of the coming of Jesus centuries after King David died, between 626 and 586 BC,

> *"The days are coming," declares the Lord, "when I will raise up to David a righteous Branch, a King who will reign wisely and do what is just and right in the land. In his days Judah will be saved and Israel will live in safety. This is the name by which he will be called: The LORD Our Righteousness."*
>
> **Jeremiah 23:5–6**
> **(Emphasis added by the author)**

Nearly nine hundred years after God spoke to Moses regarding the coming of His Son, He spoke through another prophet, Ezekiel, "My servant David will be king over them, and *they will all have one shepherd*. They will follow my laws and be careful to keep my decrees" (Ezekiel 37:24) (emphasis added by the author). Ezekiel's prophetic word was to David's descendant, the "one shepherd," who would be Jesus. To better understand, please read John 10:11, 14–16. I would quote only verses eleven and the end of sixteen, where we will find Jesus stating, "I am the good shepherd. The good shepherd lays down his life for the sheep." "There shall be one flock and one shepherd." Jesus promised He would be the shepherd to all, not only to the Jews but also to the Gentiles (non-Jewish). What a marvelous blessing! Please read John 10:11, 14–16 for a better understanding.

I noticed many times in the Scriptures that the Lord refers to King David as "My servant David." Even David, whenever he was in a conversation with the Lord, in his humility, would refer to himself as "Your servant." In fact, while I was studying 2 Samuel 7, I noticed in verses eighteen and onward that David repeated it at least nine times.

Oh, what an awesome testimony by Jesus Himself. After His death, resurrection, and ascension into heaven, He sent His message through an angel to Apostle John while he was in the Spirit

PROPHECIES ABOUT THE COMING OF JESUS

on the island of Patmos. So let us go to the last book in the Holy Bible, **"I, Jesus, have sent my angel to give you this testimony for the churches. I am the Root and the Offspring of David, and the bright Morning Star"** (Revelation 22:16). Hallelujah! Please refer to Numbers 24:17 for a better understanding of "the bright Morning Star."

Now let me go back to the Old Testament to include one more prophecy, "Therefore the Lord himself will give you a sign: The virgin will be with child and will give birth to a son, and will call him Immanuel" (Isaiah 7:14). This prophecy was fulfilled nearly seven hundred years later, and by reading Matthew 1:18–24, Luke 1:26–38; 2:1–7, you will get more in-depth knowledge on the fulfillment of these prophecies.

There was a young virgin named Mary living in Nazareth, a town in Galilee. She had been betrothed to a righteous man named Joseph, who was also a descendant of King David (please read Luke 1:26–27). God the Father, in His grace, had truly amazing plans for this teenager—not merely to be the wife of a man, but most importantly, to be the mother of God the Son, Jesus. One day, the Lord sent His angel Gabriel to Mary, and he said to her, "Rejoice, highly favored one, the Lord is with you; blessed are you among women!" (Luke 1:28, NKJV).

Naturally, the young girl became frightened as soon as she saw the heavenly host and heard the greetings from the angel. It is quite normal for people to have such a reaction when they experience the presence and the glory of God. We see in the Holy Bible many times when men fell facedown trembling (e.g., Daniel 8:16–17; Ezekiel 43:3; Revelation 1:17). The Scriptures don't tell us whether Mary fell down or remained standing. I'm sure she was overwhelmed, and yet she was coherent enough to ask questions to clarify matters. The angel encouraged her and gave her a lengthy, even more surprising message from God,

Do not be afraid, Mary, for you have found favor with God. And behold, you will conceive in your womb and bring forth a Son, and shall call His name JESUS. He will be great, and will be called the Son of the Highest; and the Lord God will give Him the throne of His father David.

Luke 1:30–32 (NKJV)
(Emphasis added by the author)

Then Mary asked the angel how she could become pregnant, for she was a virgin—never had a sexual relationship with a man. The angel replied: *"The Holy Spirit will come upon you, and the power of the Highest will overshadow you; therefore, also, that Holy One who is to be born will be called the Son of God"* (Luke 1:35, NKJV) (emphasis added by the author). The angel also informed Mary that Elizabeth, her cousin, who had been barren now in her old age, was six months pregnant with a son (who would become known as John the Baptist). The angel emphasized to Mary, "For with God nothing will be impossible" (Luke 1:37, NKJV).

Although at first the young virgin was troubled by the message, she humbled herself and was ready to do the will of God. Mary's response to the angel was, "Behold the maidservant of the Lord! Let it be to me according to your word" (Luke 1:38, NKJV). Immediately after the angel left, Mary headed to the hill country of Judea to visit her cousin, who was six months pregnant. When Elizabeth heard Mary's greetings, her baby in the womb felt the presence of the Son of God and gave a sudden strong kick; in other words, the baby jumped for joy. At that very moment, Elizabeth was filled with the Holy Spirit, and in a loud voice, she proclaimed,

Blessed are you among women [just as the angel had said to Mary], and blessed is the fruit of your womb! But why is this granted to me, that the mother of my Lord should come to me? For indeed, as soon as the

PROPHECIES ABOUT THE COMING OF JESUS

> *voice of your greeting sounded in my ears, the babe leaped in my womb for joy.*
> *[It was Elizabeth who declared to the world the very first time that Mary is the Mother of God.]*
>
> **Luke 1:42–44 (NKJV)**
> **(Emphasis added by the author)**

I would like you to have a greater understanding of the transformation that took place within Elizabeth's womb upon hearing the greetings from the Mother of God. So, I humbly ask you to read Luke 1:39–45.

Mary spent her first trimester (first three months of her pregnancy) with Elizabeth and her husband, the priest Zechariah. While there, she glorified the Lord and wrote what has become known as Mary's Magnificat. As I studied this portion of Scripture, I was astonished to know Mary was so mindful of God at her very young age. She had such wisdom, knowledge, and understanding about her Savior. It seemed that she was quite knowledgeable of the book of Psalms, the prophecies, and all of the Scriptures that had been recorded in the Old Testament up to that point. Thus, she must have been well prepared and ready to accept this huge responsibility as "the virgin mother of God's Son!" (Please read Luke 1:46–55.)

Joseph became alarmed, for he could not understand how this could be happening. He had never had relations with Mary, so he was on the verge of divorcing her without publicity (betrothal in that time among Jews was essentially the same as being married—the equivalent of a divorce would be necessary to dissolve the relationship) in order to protect her from being judged and stoned to death. This was the punishment for adultery in those days (Deuteronomy 22:23–24). But God had greater plans for him, being he would take care of the holy one, the Son of God—Jesus. He sent an angel to give Joseph assurance,

> *But after he had considered this, an angel of the Lord appeared to him in a dream and said, "Joseph, son of David, do not be afraid to take Mary home as your wife, because what is conceived in her is from the Holy Spirit. She will give birth to a son, and you are to give him the name Jesus, because he will save his people from their sins."*
>
> **Matthew 1:20–21**
> **(Emphasis added by the author)**

So, he took Mary as his wife, but he didn't have intimacy with her. (For more in-depth understanding, please read Matthew 1:18–25.)

When Mary was in her last trimester, the ruler of the Roman Empire, Caesar Augustus, sent out an order that regardless of how far away they lived, everyone must report to their own hometown in order to register for the census. Since Joseph and Mary were both descendants of King David, they traveled from Nazareth to Bethlehem in Judea (about 94 miles on a donkey), the city of David. Upon their arrival, Mary began having labor pains, but after searching for lodging, they found there were no rooms available, thus resulting in her giving birth to her firstborn Son in a stable. Mary then wrapped the newborn child in clothes and placed Him in the manger (please read Luke 2:1–7). Thus, "The Word became flesh" (incarnate) (John 1:14a).

Just as it had been prophesied by many prophets, Jesus, a descendant of King David, was born in Bethlehem over two thousand years ago. It took about one thousand years to fulfill what was promised to David, His servant, in 2 Samuel 7:12a–c, 13b–14a, 16.

In today's society, when a child is born, the family finds their house filled with visitors, such as immediate family members, neighbors, and friends. In most instances, the first visitor to the baby is its father. In Jesus' case, God the Father chose to send angels to announce the birth of His Son to the Jewish shepherds, who at that time were considered to be the lowest segment of society. Shepherding was hard labor—they would spend their lives in the field, constantly watching over their herd day and night, protecting them from wild animals and thieves. They traveled from one region to the other, guiding the flocks, in search of "green pastures and still waters" (Psalm 23:2). "They must have smelled like sheep," as my teacher made a joke in the Bible school. Shepherds had no social life, and they couldn't take a day off to observe the Sabbath as holy, for they worked so diligently in watching over their flocks, and so the teachers of the Law considered them sinners. Yet, they became the first visitors to baby Jesus! Personally, I believe this was to show the world that humans judge others by their outward appearance and status, but God from the innermost part of our hearts.

When the angels appeared to the shepherds, the glory of the Lord surrounded them, and the shepherds were frightened. The angels comforted them with the following words,

> *"Do not be afraid. I bring you good news of great joy that will be for all the people. Today in the town of David a Savior has been born to you; he is Christ the Lord. This will be a sign to you: You will find a baby wrapped in clothes and lying in a manger."*
>
> **Luke 2:10–12**
> **(Emphasis added by the author)**

> *Suddenly a great company of the heavenly hosts appeared with the angel, praising God and saying,*
> *"Glory to God in the highest, and on earth peace to men on whom his favor rests."*
>
> **Luke 2:13–14**
> **(Emphasis added by the author)**

The shepherds decided to visit the child after the angels had left them,

"Let's go to Bethlehem and see this thing that has happened, which the Lord has told us about." So they hurried off and found Mary and Joseph, and the baby, who was lying in the manger.

**Luke 2:15–16
(Emphasis added by the author)**

After they had witnessed everything exactly as they were told by the angels, the shepherds disclosed the revelation they had received from God the Father about this child. Everyone who heard their news was amazed, "But Mary treasured up all these things and pondered them in her heart" (verse 19). The shepherds praised and glorified the Lord as they went back to the field (please read Luke 2:15–20).

According to the Abrahamic covenant, the baby was circumcised on the eighth day (please read Genesis 17:10–12), and the parents named Him Jesus, as the angel Gabriel had instructed them (Luke 2:21). Although the child was the Son of God, both Mary and Joseph observed the Law of Moses, which was given by God Himself. The Law directed that if a woman had a male child as her firstborn, she would then be considered unclean for the first seven days; only on the eighth day could the child's foreskin be circumcised. As the mother continued to bleed, she was to wait a purification period of thirty-three more days before entering the sanctuary or touching anything sacred (please read Leviticus chapter 12). After those days were over, the parents brought the child to the temple in Jerusalem to present Him to the Lord and offer sacrifice (Luke 2:22–24).

In Jerusalem, there was a righteous and devout man named Simeon who had been given a promise by the Holy Spirit he would not depart from this world before seeing Christ the Savior. He was empowered by the Spirit and went into the temple as the parents brought in the baby for the ceremonies. He took the child in his

PROPHECIES ABOUT THE COMING OF JESUS

arms and praised the Lord, for he had seen the Savior of the world with his own eyes; he also blessed the parents. He said many things about the baby as well and prophesied a very special message to Mary, "And a sword will pierce your own soul too" (Luke 2:35). (Please read Luke 2:25–35 for better understanding.)

The second person who was blessed to see Jesus in the temple was Anna, the prophetess. She sought after the Lord instead of remarrying when her short seven years of married life had ended as she became a widow. Then Anna moved into the temple, where she sacrificed the rest of her life in fasting, praying, and worshiping the Lord unceasingly, even at the age of eighty-four. What a holy woman of God! As soon as she saw the child, she thanked the Lord and spoke of Him to those who had been waiting for the redeemer of Israel (Luke 2:36–38). These instances indicated that, just as Jesus told His disciples in Matthew 13:16–17 and Luke 10:23–24, there were many righteous men and women who had been waiting to see the Messiah, but the disciples themselves were tremendously blessed to have seen what they saw and heard what they heard by actually having been in His presence.

Months later, a second group of people, the Gentile magi, also known as the wise men (these men also were astronomers), came from the East (I do not know the exact location) to worship the child, besides the shepherds who were sent by God the Father to visit baby Jesus.

After seeing a special star that indicated a King had been born, they traveled probably hundreds, if not thousands, of miles to Jerusalem and went all over the city asking, "Where is the one who has been born *king of the Jews*? We saw his star in the east and have come to worship him" (Matthew 2:2, please read verses 1–2 for better understanding) (emphasis added by the author). King Herod the Great, the ruler of Judea at that time, and all the people had become very troubled upon hearing the news the magi had brought.

King Herod (a non-Jew) was concerned that the new king would succeed him, so he met with the high priest and the teachers of the Law in order to find the exact location of where Christ was to be born. (This proves that in those days, everyone, Jews, non-Jews, as well as the half-Jew like the Samaritan woman (John 4:25), were expecting the coming of Christ or the Messiah.) [How they were aware of it? They knew because the prophecies about coming of Savior through the descendant of king David, and His suffering and death were read/proclaimed every Sabbath (Acts 13:27). Please read from verse 22 onward, for better understanding. Thank You Father for revealing this to me today, 6/14/2024]. They informed him that according to prophecy, it would be in Bethlehem in Judea,

> *But you, Bethlehem Ephrathah, though you are small among the clans of Judah, out of you will come for me one who will be ruler over Israel, whose origins are from of old, from ancient times.*
>
> **Micah 5:2**
> **(Emphasis added by the author)**

It was prophesied by Micah about seven hundred years before the birth of Jesus, and it is quoted in Matthew 2:6 with slight variations in wording.

Now, when Herod secretly found out the approximate age of the child by asking the magi when this special star was revealed to them. He sent them to Bethlehem with orders to make a thorough search for Christ. He also told them to report back as soon as they found Him so he could go and worship as well, although his intention was to kill the baby.

As the magi started their journey from Herod's palace, the star, which they saw in the East, guided their way. This was no accident but the work of Almighty God. When the star came to rest over the house (notice, the baby Jesus was no longer in the manger, but in a

PROPHECIES ABOUT THE COMING OF JESUS

house), where the child was with His mother, Mary, they all bowed down to worship Him. The magi presented Jesus with gold, frankincense, and myrrh (please read Matthew 2:1–11). Gold symbolized His kingship, frankincense symbolized His high priesthood, and myrrh symbolized His death. Years after I wrote the above, the Holy Spirit revealed to me why God the Father chose to send both Jews (shepherds) and the Gentiles (magi) to visit baby Jesus. That was to show the world that He sent His Son not only to save the lost sheep of Israel but the whole world.

In response to a warning they received from the Lord, the magi returned home rather than reporting back to Herod as they had been commanded to do. When Herod realized that he had been outsmarted by the magi, he became enraged and put out an order for all male children two years old and younger (the age determined by the information he received from the magi) to be killed (please read Matthew 2:12 and 16). This would fulfill what was prophesied by Jeremiah in his book 31:15; please read for your understanding. God Almighty sent His angel to Joseph with instructions for him to escape to Egypt with the child and His mother (Matthew 2:13–14). Although it was the middle of the night, this obedient servant immediately got up (I imagine, woke up his young wife), picked up the baby, and started on the journey. In this day and age, with all of our modern conveniences, it would be impossible to comprehend the extent of the struggle Joseph must have gone through in order to lead a donkey that carried Mary and Jesus on a trip that could have taken days, weeks, or even months.

After Herod's death, the angel of the Lord instructed Joseph to bring the young child and His mother back to Israel, but this time, they settled in Galilee, in a town called Nazareth, for Herod's son was the ruler in Judea (Matthew 2:19–23). Father God did all this not only because of His love for His Son but for all mankind from generation to generation—an unconditional and everlasting love (agape). It is interesting to notice that although God the Father instructed Joseph to take Mary as his wife, the Lord never addressed Mary as his wife. He always said, "Child and his mother"! That made me wonder if they ever lived as an ordinary married couple!

"And Jesus grew in wisdom and stature, and in favor with God and men" (Luke 2:52). This Gospel writer gave us clear evidence of it with an astonishing event that took place in Jesus' boyhood life. Every year, the parents went to the Jerusalem temple for the Passover feast, and when Jesus was twelve years old, they took Him along with them. On the way back home after the feast, somehow, the child got separated; the parents did not realize their Son was missing until after a day's journey. Since they couldn't find Him among their friends and relatives who traveled with them, they returned to Jerusalem, and after a diligent search for the boy, on the third day,

> *They found Him in the temple courts, sitting among the teachers [who were proficient in prophecies and Laws], listening to them and asking them questions. Everyone who heard him was amazed at his understanding and his answers.*
>
> **Luke 2:46–47**
> **(Emphasis added by the author)**

Boy Jesus must have given them divinely brilliant answers!

Most likely, they were discussing the coming of Messiah, for in those days, everyone was waiting on Him; Jesus probably even corrected them, who knows! His parents were astonished when they found Him sitting among those scholars. (Please read Luke 2:41–48.)

From the age of twelve, there is no further documentation about Jesus' life until He began His public ministry.

Since writing this book (2008–2014), I have drawn closer than ever and grown deeper in my relationship and faith with God. Let

PROPHECIES ABOUT THE COMING OF JESUS

me reveal to you that chapter three, "The Prophecies about the Coming of Jesus (the Messiah) and Their Fulfillments," was the most difficult chapter of all.

Although I collected the data for this book in 2008, I only knew three prophecies about the coming of Jesus. One was God revealing to Moses that He would raise up a prophet like him. Second one: God made a covenant with David that after his death, He would raise up his offspring to succeed him. These two prophecies I studied in Bible school. The third one I had also heard spoken by many priests over the years; God revealed to Isaiah that a virgin would give birth to a Son, and He would be called Immanuel.

In 2011, my writer, Carolyn, and I got together to write this chapter, but I was not able to tell her anything more than what I had in the original manuscript; therefore, I moved forward to the next chapter.

By the spring of 2013, Carolyn and I rejoiced, thinking the book had been completed, but as I searched this chapter, I felt there was no flow or quality to it. My heart was greatly troubled by this. I chose to take a break to spend some time with God. Alone and brokenhearted in my prayer room, I asked the Lord to speak and guide me as to how to write His book. Daily, in my desperation, I cried out and asked God the Father to show me the prophecies written regarding the coming of His Son, and I would open the Bible, graciously He would direct my eyes, heart, and fingers to the appropriate books, passages, and messages. This may be a little difficult for you to believe, but this is what I experienced.

Whenever I drove back home from my writer's, mostly after midnight, I would praise and thank God for each day's accomplishment. I would never fail to ask God, "Am I doing the right thing?" or "Is it pleasing to You, my Lord?" In prayer, many times, as I woke up in the morning, He would put new thoughts in my mind, and I would take it back to my writer. I would tell her the way God wanted it written, and she would never fail to comply.

It was routine for me to listen to the Word of God on a tape recorder, especially when I walked alone in the park. On June 5th, 2013, while listening to the book of Revelation, I suddenly heard Jesus say, **"I am the Root and the Offspring of David"** (Revelation 22:16). My heart jumped with joy for the Lord Himself confirmed to me the most needed information at the perfect time! I felt He was pleased with the prophecies written so far, Him being from the royal line of David. The Almighty Himself gave me the confirmation that He is "the Root and the Offspring of David." By the grace and mercy of God, we were able to complete this chapter, in fact, the whole book, by early 2014. But there was much more work that needed to be done for me since Carolyn chose to move to Texas to be with her husband in the spring of 2014. And the Lord called her to be with Him in 2019.

CHAPTER 4:

MY EXPERIENCE AS A CHRISTIAN

Saint Thomas, one of the twelve apostles of Jesus Christ, came to the southern part of India (today's Kerala State) in AD 52. After hearing him preach the gospel, many Hindus converted to Christianity. He established seven and a half churches in various areas. Saint Thomas was able to complete seven of them, but for the eighth one, "he marked the location only by placing a cross there. For whatever reason, the work was undone." I was able to obtain this information from a priest who studied Indian church history. The apostle was martyred in AD 72 in Madras, India.

I was truly blessed not only to have been born into one of those traditional Christian families but also to have had godly parents, especially my mother. She was the driving force behind all the Bible reading, hymn singing, and praying that we did early every morning and before dinner each evening. We not only went to church and Sunday school weekly, but we observed Lent and attended mostly all the holy day services as well.

Due to my background, I naturally assumed I would continue with the same religious practices in my married life. But after my wedding, it seemed everything suddenly fell apart. My husband, Simon, was from the same Christian denomination—the Indian

Orthodox Church—and yet church attendance was of little or no importance to him; in fact, each time we went, it seemed as if we were passing through a war zone. In the very first year of our marriage, I had to miss the Easter and Christmas services and many Sunday services at our church due to his resistance. Believe it or not, in the midst of all this turmoil and confusion, we never went to bed before reading the Scriptures and praying together.

We had two children within five years, and as they approached school age, I felt a burden and urgency that they be brought up the same way I had been. I knew that we were moving away from the Lord, so I wholeheartedly prayed for a job that would let me work Monday through Friday from 9 a.m. to 5 p.m., which would allow me to be home with the family for evening prayer and Bible reading. I also wanted to be able to take the children to church and Sunday school each week. I promised God that I would teach Sunday school if He would simply provide the right job for me. In less than two years, I got that job! As a registered nurse, I had been making $23,000 annually, and to take the new job, I sacrificed and took a $5,000 pay cut. Simon voiced some opposition to making the change, but I paid him no mind because God was my priority—not the money. Shortly after assuming my new position, I kept my promise to God, and we parents adapted the daily evening prayers in English for the sake of our children. These were truly my happy days!

In the mid-1980s, I was given the opportunity to teach the little children's Sunday school class in my church, which I enjoyed very much. Then, in the mid-1990s, I began teaching the higher grades. It didn't take long for me to realize that my students knew more about the Scriptures than I did. Although I had read the entire Bible two or three times in my life, I had never studied or memorized the Word of God as the students had been compelled to do. I found myself feeling embarrassed and uncomfortable, for I realized that I hardly knew the Bible. I felt ashamed of myself, for, in my mind, I wasn't worthy to call myself a Christian, a follower of Jesus Christ. I reminded myself of the Ethiopian eunuch who was an important official in charge of the treasury of Candace, the queen of Ethiopia. After worshipping the Lord in Jerusalem, he was traveling back home by chariot and reading from the book of Isaiah,

> *He was oppressed and afflicted, yet he did not open his mouth; he was led like a lamb to the slaughter, and as a sheep before her shearers is silent, so he did not open his mouth. By oppression and judgment he was taken away. And who can speak of his descendants? For he was cut off from the land of the living; for the transgression of my people he was stricken.*
>
> **Isaiah 53:7–8**
> **(Emphasis added by the author)**

(This is quoted in Acts 8:32–33.)

Suddenly, Phillip, one of the seven deacons (Acts 6:3–6), under the direction of the angel of the Lord (please read Acts 8:26–29), approached the eunuch and asked him if he understood what he was reading. Although he was educated and intelligent, he answered, *"How can I understand unless someone explains it to me?"* (Acts 8:31a, NCV) (emphasis added by the author). The eunuch immediately invited him into the chariot, and Phillip began to explain all about the passages, about whom it was written and preached Jesus' suffering, crucifixion, resurrection, and ascension (Acts 8:35). The eunuch couldn't wait to be baptized after clearly understanding the Scriptures and believing that Jesus was the Son of God. This is a perfect example of the difference between reading the Bible and studying. When we study the Scriptures, transformation takes place in our hearts, and the Holy Spirit will guide us to the right path. The eunuch accepted Jesus as his Savior and was baptized by Phillip (please read Acts 8:30–39).

Over the years, I found myself becoming more and more frustrated because I was unable to understand the Word of God. The Bible seemed like an ocean to me, too deep and wide. For example, when Jesus was tempted by the devil, He told the devil, "It is written: 'Man does not live on bread alone, but on every word that comes from the mouth of God'" (Matthew 4:4). I would ask myself, "Where is it written? Is it in the Bible or somewhere else?" I simply could not connect the Old Testament to the New Testament or one book to the other—not even one verse to another. Like the Ethiopian eunuch, I felt I needed someone to explain it to me. At this point, I knew I needed to go to Bible school, where I could sit in a classroom and let a teacher help me comprehend it all. I immediately started asking around about Bible schools. By the end of 1998, I heard about a school in mid-town Manhattan, the New York School of the Bible, and I started in the spring of 1999.

As I looked at the school's brochure, I was thrilled when I saw "How to Study the Bible" listed among their available classes. This was the first course I took in the spring of 1999. It was exactly what I needed, and it happened to be the most difficult class, as well.

Studying the Scriptures with that group of scholars taught me that it is vitally important to have a good study Bible. I needed one with the best possible references, the kind that actually connected the Old and New Testaments together, book to book, and even passage to passage. Some other valuable tools that are helpful for in-depth study are maps, which give us names of locations, along with a better understanding of them and clearer pictures of the surroundings. It's also very important to have abundant and accurate commentaries, along with a scripturally sound Bible dictionary and concordance. For deep, effectual study, we should first read the King James or Authorized Version, a time-tested version translated faithfully from the original Hebrew, Aramaic, and Greek, renowned for its lack of theological bias and its formal equivalence to the original languages. But if you have a problem understanding that one, select a translation that is more easily understood. Truly, I had never heard of a study Bible or any other translation except the King James until I joined this school.

Now, I think it is very important to take this time and especially the opportunity to thank all the biblical scholars who put their heart and soul together and worked so hard as the Holy Spirit guided them to make these study Bibles available to the public, especially to people like me. I would also like to thank all my teachers at the New York School of the Bible and its faculty, for without these special people, today, ten years later, I would still be struggling to know what the Bible is all about. My request to everyone, especially the theologians and biblical scholars who read this book, is to correct me if you find any content in this book that contradicts the Holy Bible, please. I will treasure your comments, teachings, and corrections. Thanks for your kindness. I thank God Almighty for guiding me throughout my life and quenching my thirst for the living Word of God. It seems as if I can't get enough of God's Word; the more I study, the more and more I want to know, and the closer I feel to Him, and my faith just grows and grows. It has come to the point where I realize that I am nothing, and He is everything, and I can't do and don't want to do *anything* without Him.

In my earlier life, I thought I was doing everything religiously right, and yet, bringing up the children and making sure they got the right education was a great challenge in my life. Especially knowing that in my culture these days, education is the number one priority; people with the least education are looked down on the most. So, as a parent, you are responsible for making sure that each of your children receives at least the equivalent of a baccalaureate degree. Thus, it was only natural for me and my husband to encourage and expect our children to complete their education in a timely manner. Our son, Simon Jr., accomplished the task successfully, but our daughter, Maureen, not only quit college three times by 1999, but she was least interested in furthering her education and achieving a college degree.

When Maureen was a toddler, she was so thin that we were quite concerned, especially when one of her father's friends from India visited us and asked if we ever fed the poor child. So, we tried feeding her all the wrong things due to our ignorance of proper nutrition. There were times I would buy a pizza and eat only the crust while giving Maureen the toppings. Simon, in an effort to correct Maureen's low weight, would make the child drink cod liver oil. As she grew, Simon brought home larger and larger quantities of pastries, chocolates, cakes, and ice cream. We all began eating way too much fast food and drinking far too many sodas. Gradually, Maureen began putting on the pounds. It wasn't long before our daughter became overweight. Some of our friends here in America would tell us it was merely baby fat and that soon it would go away. But she has struggled with the problem ever since. By the grace of God, being overweight did not discourage her from being in public places.

After she quit college, I encouraged Maureen to take some computer classes, which she did, and she got a full-time job that paid $15,000 per year with hardly any benefits. It truly devastated me; my thinking was, how could she live independently and survive? Because even with three times more than her earnings, I was in a financial struggle at the same period of time.

Like any other mother, I wanted only the best for my child. Months later, I heard about the New York State jobs available for "keyboard specialists," but first, one must pass the civil service examination. When I told Maureen to sit for the exam, she flatly refused and said, "No, you're pushing me too much." Maureen is like the story Jesus spoke in Matthew 21:28–31; a father had two sons, he said to the oldest one to go to the vineyard and work, he responded "no" he would not, then the father approached his second son and told the same, and he agreed to go. But you know who did the will of the father? The one who said "no." Likewise, Maureen changed her mind, passed the civil-service examination, and got the New York State job. This gave me great relief because she would get benefits such as health insurance, sick time, and earned annual leave, besides the increase in salary by $6,000–7,000 per year.

While Maureen was working for the state, one of my church members asked me, "Why don't you send your daughter to the Chubb Institute of Technology for computer studies? Because the people who graduate from there are making $50,000 per year." This sounded very good to me, and I thanked the person so very much for her generous heart. Well, again, I approached my daughter. With much encouragement, she joined Chubb Institute of Technology and received a diploma in computer networking in 2001. But unfortunately, too many foreigners came in, and either they took up many of the computer jobs or they were given preference over American graduates, so a position was not available for her at that time.

Only later in life, after I made some progress in understanding the Word of God, I realized that all I did was according to my will and my desires. My greatest guilt of all, I didn't let my child pursue her preference; instead, I persuaded her to take up the profession that I thought would be better for her, and it ended up in disaster. With all the religious life I was leading, I never asked God to guide or lead us to the right path. This is to say, I had no relationship or intimacy with Jesus, knew only to ask for material things, not knowing if I cast all my burden on Jesus' shoulder (as He said in Matthew 11:28), He would have carried it easily and handled it better. I failed because of my ignorance of Jesus' teachings and lacked complete faith in Him.

Although I had memorized most of the written prayers without understanding and prayed mornings and evenings from my younger age, my heart was still void. Whatever prayer I said from my lips was coming from the head, not from my heart. But one thing I do recall praying from my heart for a few years was, "Lord, give me wisdom, knowledge, and a generous heart," even though I did not study the Proverbs, I heard and read the story about King Solomon. When he asked for wisdom, God gave it to him abundantly, and he used it wisely to judge the two prostitutes when they brought him a dead child and a living one (please read 1 Kings 3:5–28). Please don't read me wrong; I do not disown those written prayers. Only later in life did I realize that the spiritual fathers who wrote those prayers knew the Bible very thoroughly and lived an intimate life with the Lord; otherwise, they would not have written such faithful prayers. There are times I feel like I am unworthy to say some of those powerful prayers, for I did not apply them to myself and felt as though I was lying to God.

My gravest concern was, "Who is going to marry my daughter under these circumstances?" Maureen has many wonderful qualities, but unfortunately, in our society, she lacked two of the most important things: a slim figure and a bachelor's degree or a professional job. As my child's problems mounted, I became weak, did not know what to do, and finally led me to depression in 2002. If you would kindly go to chapter seven in this book and read "The Fulfillment of the Prophecies Regarding Jesus' Suffering," you will understand how my Savior miraculously healed me from this illness and made me strong.

Maureen's situation influenced me to go to the chapel daily at my new workplace from the beginning of February 2003, where on my knees, I prayed and cried out to God for her, "Lord, do not let the child suffer due to her parents' ignorance." I had no idea that very prayer would result in a life-changing experience for me, a miracle so great that I can hardly express it in words. On May 12, as usual, I went to the chapel and noticed in the front pew a young lady kneeling and praying to the Lord with her arms lifted toward heaven. I was extremely happy to witness such a scene. I immediately started to pray for her, "God, please bless her." I stayed in the back of the chapel and resumed the prayer for my daughter.

As the woman was about to leave, she approached and asked me, "Are you a Christian?"

My instant reply was, "If I weren't a Christian, I wouldn't be here."

Then she asked me gently, "Can I sit with you?"

At this, we both sat down on the bench, and she asked me, "Do you have a daughter?"

I said yes, and then I was completely overwhelmed by her response.

She said, "God the Father told me to tell you, 'I know you are troubled about your daughter, and I'll take care of that.'"

At this, we thanked and praised the Lord in joy and gladness. The weight that had been on my shoulders, neck, and chest, at last, was gone. Oh, what a miraculous peace! This entire experience helped me realize that God is still using prophets today, just as they were used in the early biblical days. Since then, in my heart, I have called this place "my Father's house," not a chapel.

God is so good and totally amazing. I went straight from being in agonizing prayer daily to having a message delivered to me by God Himself. He chose to use a stranger who became my lifelong sister in Christ and my prophetess, Norma Perez.

Four months later, Maureen enrolled in a different college (St. Joseph's College, Brooklyn, from where I graduated), and after a few years, she received her degree. She is currently working on losing weight. Now, last but not least, my husband and I are praying for the Lord to bring both Maureen and Simon godly Christian mates. Also, we pray they will raise their children in the nurture and admonition of the Lord.

As Norma had advised me, I began spending more time in the Scriptures and continuously talking to God the Father, for He loves that. Actually, God had been speaking to me, but I was not in a spiritual capacity to acknowledge that it was Him until, one day, my prophetess confirmed to me that, "God has been speaking to you, but you didn't realize it was the Lord." Since then, I have been paying closer attention to Him; yes, today, God still speaks to me through the prophetess or some other prophet, but more often, He speaks to me directly. Truly, I have tasted that He is an awesome God!

On November 30, 2006, at 5:30 p.m., after eighteen years of menopause, I began to bleed. I was not at all in panic or afraid, but my colleagues were truly concerned, and right away, one of them made an appointment with the chief gynecologist in the same hospital. Within three days, all the necessary work up was done, and I waited for the results. Prior to this, I had already planned for a vacation and booked the air ticket to go to Atlanta to be with my husband during the Christmas and New Year's celebrations, for he had already retired in Georgia.

I reported everything to Simon and told him, "Don't worry, there's no need to come to New York even if I have to have surgery (thinking I might have cancer). I can manage with the children here; take care of Buddy and Rocky (our loving dogs)." While waiting for the results of the workup, as usual, I went to my Father's house (the chapel), but this time, it was for me. I was courageous enough to go all the way to the front pew, very next to the altar. There, I knelt down, and as I was praying, the Word came to my heart, saying, "I am the Shepherd." When I told my prophetess about this, she explained to me that it means, "God is your Shepherd, and you are His sheep. He will protect you and guide you."

Surely, she was right; the bleeding had been tapering off as if

MY EXPERIENCE AS A CHRISTIAN

I was having the menstrual period. On my second office visit, the doctor told me all the results came out negative but advised me to come back in six months for a follow-up. Certainly, I kept the appointment; the gynecologist didn't even have to examine me since I didn't have any further bleeding. The doctor told me that I was in good health and discharged me.

It took me a while to realize that the Lord was teaching me a lesson through this experience. As I mentioned earlier, I prayed twice daily, and Psalm 51, King David's repentance, was included in our morning prayers; without the understanding of it, I used to recite this every morning. Once I went to Bible school, the teacher taught this Psalm so thoroughly, and when it came to verse 14a, "Save me from blood guilt, O God." He explained, "David was pleading to God to stop the bloodshed from his family because two of his sons were murdered, one by his own son and the other by his own army." After learning this, I asked myself, "Why am I praying this portion of the Psalm? My family didn't have any problem." Well, the Lord surely taught me a lesson through this post-menopausal bleeding; the circumstances may change, but His words will never change.

If the Lord had not given me the title and guided me through the writing process from beginning to end, I could never have imagined or attempted to write this book; each day, I found myself crying out to God, "Lord, You know that I don't know how to write, but everything is possible with You."

Then an encouraging thought came to my mind, and I said to the Lord, "The apostles John and Peter were fishermen, and You made them write Your books. So, help me, Father—teach me, instruct me, and guide me (Psalm 32:8) in the way in which You want me to write Your book." For there are times—days, weeks, and even months that go by without anything being written. He would then remind me of some Scriptures that encouraged me to start writing again. For example, Jesus said,

> Not everyone who says to me, 'Lord, Lord,' will enter the kingdom of heaven, but only he who does the will of my Father who is in heaven. Many will say to me on that day, 'Lord, Lord, did we not prophesy in your name and in your name drive out demons and perform many miracles?' Then I will tell them plainly, 'I never knew you. Away from me, you evildoers!'
>
> **Matthew 7:21–23**
> **(Emphasis added by the author)**

Just the thought of Jesus saying those words to me is terrifying!

Another time, God reminded me of the parable of the servant who received five talents, who went at once and put his money to work and turned it into ten talents. Another servant received two talents, and he worked it out and made it into four, but the one who only received one talent was a nonproductive servant, for he dug a hole in the ground and buried it, producing nothing. I promised the Lord that I would never be like the unproductive servant and bury my talent but that I would always use it for His honor and glory. I want to be a faithful servant like those who multiplied their talents. (Please read Matthew 25:14–30.)

My constant prayer is, "With the talent that You gave me, oh Lord, You will mold and make this into a book that will be read by tens of thousands and draw many unto You. I pray, too, that many will be motivated to study the Scriptures and that they will taste and see what a truly awesome, loving, kind, compassionate, merciful, and forgiving God You are!"

CHAPTER 5:

WHAT WAS THE PURPOSE OF HIS COMING?

Why would the Creator of all lower Himself from the highest position and become like one of His own creations? He had a mission to accomplish! And it all began after Adam and Eve, the first man and the first woman, His best friends, fell into the devil's scheme. Let's go to Genesis, the first book in the Bible, 1:1–25, to learn how God created the whole universe and everything in it. Everything came into being simply by His spoken word. When He said, "Let there be such and such," immediately, there it was! Whereas if we read further, we learn that humanity was created in a very special way, in God's own image and His likeness, which means we are able to think rationally, keep a personal relationship with God, and be morally right with the Creator, "The LORD God formed a man from the dust of the ground and breathed into his nostrils the breath of life [God's spirit which we all share], and the man became a living being" (Genesis 2:7). God gave him the name Adam. When God decided that it was not good for the man to be alone, He created the woman, but in a totally different and unique way,

> *So the LORD God caused the man to fall into a deep sleep [like being in general anesthesia]; and while*

he was sleeping, he took one of the man's ribs and closed up the place with flesh [a major surgery took place]. Then the LORD God made a woman from the rib he had taken out of the man, and he brought her to the man.

**Genesis 2:21–22
(Emphasis added by the author)**

Upon seeing her, Adam said, "This is now bone of my bones and flesh of my flesh; she shall be called 'woman,' for she was taken out of man" (2:23). He later named her Eve, for she would become the mother of all humanity. (Please read Genesis 2:21–24; 3:20.)

The Lord placed Adam and Eve in the Garden of Eden, a perfect place, a paradise, with an unimaginable variety of trees, shrubs, and plants that produced every type of fruit/food. God gave Adam an assignment, which was to work in the garden and to be its caretaker, for that was his reasonable service to the Lord. Adam was given the freedom to eat from every tree in the garden except one, and that was "the tree of the knowledge of good and evil" (Genesis 2:17). In 3:3, we notice this tree was in the center of the garden. He was strictly warned that if he ate fruit from the forbidden tree, he would definitely die on the spot (Genesis 2:16–17). The word "death" used here is speaking of sudden spiritual death, not physical death; sin, which causes separation from God, is also referred to as the "fall of man." The Lord gave Adam and Eve free will, which meant they had the freedom to choose divine wisdom or their own desire.

One day, the devil came in the form of a serpent and was so brilliant he had no problem convincing Eve that if she ate the forbidden fruit, she would never die but would be like God, knowing both good and evil. The devil himself wanted to be like the Most High God (Isaiah 14:14), so he put his thought in the innocent victim's mind; thus, Eve not only tasted of the fruit, but she also gave to her husband. Sadly, Adam, like his wife, abused his free will (please read Genesis 3:1–6). The tragedy of it all is that they both knew (Genesis 3:3) if they ate the forbidden fruit, they would instantly die. As soon as they ate that fruit, their eyes were opened. They realized they were naked, and they heard the sound of the Lord walking in the garden, and they hid behind a tree from Him (Genesis 3:7–8).

Then, God called out to Adam and asked, "Where are you?" (verse 9, NKJV).

Adam answered, "I heard Your voice in the garden [walking], and I was afraid because I was naked; and I hid myself" (3:10, NKJV).

According to verse eight in the same chapter, it seems that it was routine for the Lord to visit His friends late in the evening. Now, the same sound of footsteps that once had been so comforting and peaceful had suddenly become frightening due to disobedience.

God asked Adam, "Who told you that you were naked? Have you eaten from the tree of which I commanded you that you should not eat?" (Genesis 3:11, NKJV).

Instead of repentance, here comes the "chain of blame:" The man blames it on God and the woman; then Eve blames it on the serpent because it had deceived her. Then God turned and cursed the serpent and told him,

> *Because you have done this, "Cursed are you above all the livestock and all the wild animals! You will crawl on your belly and you will eat dust all the days of your life. And I will put enmity between you and the woman, and between your offspring and hers; he will crush your head, and you will strike his heel."*
>
> **Genesis 3:14–15**
> **(Emphasis added by the author)**

Please read Genesis chapter three and focus on verse fifteen, for this is the good news, the first time God ever preached to the world. The woman God spoke about was the same one of whom Isaiah later prophesied, "The virgin shall be with child." That same woman, Virgin Mary, would later become the mother of Jesus. Her offspring and the serpent would always be enemies, but Jesus would be victorious, for striking the heel is nothing compared to crushing the head, which is sudden death.

God knew that if Adam and Eve remained in the Garden of Eden, they would be tempted to eat from the "tree of life" and live forever in their sinful state. God didn't want them to suffer, so He drove them out of the Garden. He then told Adam that until his death, he would do hard labor in the ground in order to have food to eat, and when he died, he would return to the dust from which he was formed (3:17–19). Due to Adam's momentary act of rebellion, all of mankind has been eternally separated from God. His sin caused suffering, hard labor, sickness, hunger, thirst, and ultimately physical death to enter the world. Because Eve defied God, she caused all women to suffer severe pain during labor and childbirth (Genesis 3:16).

Our God is so loving, forgiving, compassionate, and all-knowing that He didn't want to abolish all of mankind; in fact, He wanted to bring the fallen human race back to be with Him in paradise. This is the very reason why Jesus came to this world,

> *For God so loved the world [all people] that he gave his one and only Son, that whoever believes in him shall not perish but have eternal life. For God did not send his Son into the world to condemn the world, but to save the world through him.*
>
> **John 3:16–17**
> **(Emphasis added by the author)**

WHAT WAS THE PURPOSE OF HIS COMING?

Can you imagine how God must have felt when Adam chose to be disobedient and, in turn, broke their close fellowship? His desire to restore that relationship with all mankind was so great that He was even willing to sacrifice His one and only Son. And Apostle Paul wrote, "But when the time had fully come, God sent his Son, born of a woman, born under law, to redeem those under law, that we might receive the full rights of sons" (Galatians 4:4–5). To learn about the miraculous birth of Jesus, please refer to chapter 3, "The Prophecies about the Coming of Jesus (the Messiah) and Their Fulfillment."

Jesus started His public ministry at about the age of thirty, after being baptized by John the Baptist (Luke 3:21–23). That baptism must have been the most profound experience for John, for although he opposed baptizing Jesus when He approached him, he had no choice but to be submissive. Imagine the creation (John) placing his right hand on the head of the Creator and immersing Him in the water of the Jordan River! Remember, John had told the world the one who was coming after him was greater than him, and he was unworthy to carry His sandals; as he was humbled, God exalted him to baptize His Son (please read Matthew 3:11–15).

Just as Jesus came up out of the water praying,

> *Heaven was opened and the Holy Spirit descended on him in bodily form like a dove [anointing Him, Acts 10:38]. And a voice came from heaven: "You are my Son, whom I love; with you I am well pleased."*
>
> **Luke 3:21–22**
> **(Emphasis added by the author)**

(Also recorded in Mark 1:9–11; Matthew 3:16–17.)

Here, we see the presence of God the Father, God the Son, and God the Holy Spirit (the Trinity) at the same time. [Years after I wrote about Jesus' baptism, a thought came into my heart: had not

Jesus willingly been baptized by His creation, would we have ever known there is a Triune God: the Father, the Son, and the Holy Spirit?] Soon, Jesus was led by the Holy Spirit into the desert, where He fasted for forty days and forty nights in preparation for His public ministry. Naturally, by the time the fasting was finished, He was weak and hungry. What better time could the devil have chosen to tempt Him? The devil approached Jesus and said, "If you are the Son of God, tell these stones to become bread" (Matthew 4:3).

Then Jesus replied, "It is written: 'Man does not live on bread alone, but on every word that comes from the mouth of God'" (Matthew 4:4) (which is quoted from Deuteronomy 8:3). Although the devil failed at his first attempt, he aggressively continued with two more, and yet all three were utter failures (please read Matthew 4:2–11). Here, the war (animosity) between the devil and Christ (the woman's offspring) began, just as God the Father foretold in Genesis 3:15. By Jesus' actions, He demonstrated to us how vitally important it is to fast, pray, study, and meditate on the Word of God in order to keep ourselves from being polluted by the world and to be equipped and ready to overcome the forces of evil.

Jesus began preaching in Capernaum, where the two tribes, Zebulun and Naphtali, lived (they were the two sons of Israel/Jacob, amongst the twelve). This land was allotted to their descendants by God Himself when the Israelites returned from Egypt (please read Joshua 19:10–16, 32–39 and pay attention to verse 34). And it was near the Jordan, thus fulfilled the prophecy of Isaiah 9:1–2 (must read; this is quoted in Matthew 4:15–16), with a message similar to that of John the Baptist, "Repent, for the kingdom of heaven is near" (Matthew 4:17). (Also recorded in Mark 1:15.) And the Lord is telling us the same today, for He will be back.

Jesus knew that His ministry would last only a few short years, He selected twelve men as His disciples. It seems so amazing that these men, regardless of what they were doing when He called, dropped everything immediately and followed Him (please read Matthew 4:18–22, 9:9). He wanted to maintain a close relationship with them. As the Father and Son are One, they too would be one in Him—not only the disciples but all those who believe in Christ through their gospel message. That was Jesus' prayer for the whole world (John 17:20–23).

It must have been a major decision-making day, for Jesus had a large crowd of disciples following Him (Luke 6:17), and out of them, He needed only twelve, one to betray Him and the other eleven to be His witnesses throughout the world as apostles. Jesus made the decision only after a long night's prayer to His Father in heaven (Luke 6:12–13). The names of the disciples were Simon Peter, his brother Andrew, James, son of Zebedee, his brother John (all four of them were fishermen), Philip, Bartholomew (Nathaniel), Matthew (also known as Levi, a tax collector), Thomas, James, son of Alphaeus, Thaddaeus (Judas, son of James in Luke), Simon the Zealot, and Judas Iscariot (these names are recorded in Matthew 10:2–4; Mark 3:14–19; Luke 6:13–16). All of them were Jews, God's covenant people, and they sacrificed their lives for Jesus Christ, except Judas Iscariot. The disciples not only lived and died for the Lord but for us as well. Today, had it not been for them, we would not have any knowledge of God or who He is. Every believer should have that same willingness to be obedient to God's call.

According to the Gospel of Matthew 5:3–12, Jesus began to equip the disciples to be His witnesses throughout the world by teaching them the Beatitudes, which consisted of eight characteristics of the citizens of God's kingdom, two of which are listed below, "Blessed are the poor in spirit, for theirs is the kingdom of heaven" (verse 3). These are the ones who have learned to put God on the throne of their heart. They know that they are totally dependent on the Savior, and they feel they are nothing without Him.

Here, "blessed" is used with a spiritual connotation rather than a worldly one, which is short-lived, and it means joyful or happy.

"Blessed are those who are persecuted because of righteousness, for theirs is the kingdom of heaven" (verse 10). Most of the disciples were martyred because of their beliefs and their teachings. Just as in the biblical days, there are Christians in this world today who make a conscious decision to stand up for their faith in Jesus Christ. Although they are being abused, threatened, falsely accused, and even, at times, put to death, they know that God has their reward waiting for them when they get home to heaven.

Let's go to Matthew chapters five, six, and seven, where we find that Jesus had noticed a large crowd following Him and had gone up to a mountainside to deliver His message, which became known as the famous "Sermon on the Mount." Since the Lord was constantly teaching various subjects, who knows how many days and nights He might have spent with them, covering all the lessons! (For Jesus said in another situation, in Mark 8:1–2, the crowd was with Him for three days.) We know that the people were not bored because, at the end of His teaching, the Scripture says, "The crowds were amazed at his teaching, because he taught as one who had authority, and not as their teachers of the law" (7:28–29). Remember, Jesus knew everything, and He used His divine power, for He was both Man and God at the same time.

On this same occasion, Jesus taught the importance of having complete faith in Him. As He was coming down from the mountainside, "A man with leprosy came and knelt before him and said, 'Lord, if you are willing, you can make me clean'" (Matthew 8:2). It's important to know that in those days, people with leprosy were considered to be ceremonially unclean, and therefore, those persons would have been isolated (Leviticus 13); however, our King of kings did not hesitate a moment, but instantly reached out His hand and touched the man and said, "'I am willing …Be clean!' Immediately he was cured of his leprosy" (Matthew 8:3). What an awesome confirmation of this leper's faith. He had no doubt in his mind that Jesus could heal him completely, which is why he said, "Lord, if you're willing, you can make me clean." Jesus knew the man's heart and how strong his faith was. If all believers would ask God to increase their faith up to that level, they would begin to see miracles happening in their lives as well.

Now let's look at a couple of lessons Jesus taught during his Sermon on the Mount besides the Beatitudes,

> *Therefore everyone who hears these words of mine and puts them into practice is like a wise man who built his house on the rock. The rain came down, the streams rose, and the winds blew and beat against that house; yet it did not fall, because it had its foundation on the rock.*
>
> **Matthew 7:24–25**
> **(Emphasis added by the author)**

Each time Jesus uses the word "rock" in these verses, He is referring to Himself/God. Not only in the New Testament but also in the Old Testament, addressing God as "Rock." Hannah said in her prayer, "There is no Rock like our God" (1 Samuel 2:2c). King David addressed God as his Rock, the fortress, the deliverer, the stronghold, the Savior in Psalm 18:2; 28:1; and 62:2, and again, I have noticed in Isaiah 17:10, the prophet also had addressed God as Savior and Rock.

Jesus continued His teachings and said,

> *But everyone who hears these words of mine and does not put them into practice is like a foolish man who built his house on sand. The rain came down, the streams rose, and the winds blew and beat against that house, and it fell with a great crash.*
>
> **Matthew 7:26–27**
> **(Emphasis added by the author)**

An example for the second part of this lesson is illustrated in the Bible; please read Mark 10:17–25. One day, a wealthy young man who was curious to know how to obtain eternal life, rushed to Jesus, knelt before Him, and asked, "What must I do to inherit eternal life?" (Mark 10:17). He also let Him know that from his boyhood he had been obedient to all the commandments. Jesus loved him when He heard it and instructed the young man, "One thing you lack" (verse 21), sell all his possessions and distribute them to the poor; thus, first, build the treasure in heaven, then follow Him. Unlike all His disciples who left everything to follow Christ upon their callings, this young man's heart was troubled, for he couldn't give up his huge wealth in exchange for eternal life. Jesus said, "For where your treasure is, there your heart will be also" (Matthew 6:21). What a perfect example for all of us; take it to heart! Unfortunately, because this young man's foundation was built upon the sand (the world) and its instability instead of upon the Rock, he walked away dejected. What a great crash! He was just one step away from inheriting the Lord's kingdom!

Just as in times past, today we can see many broken families, divorces, same-sex marriages, ruined business partnerships, and—saddest of all—even some failing churches. All these failures take place because people build their foundation on the sand instead of on the Rock/Jesus.

As I was studying the first part of the lesson (Matthew 7:24–25), God heavily burdened my heart with two thoughts: one was that of the strong faith of the Canaanite woman, and the other was the faith of Father Abraham.

A Canaanite woman came to Jesus, crying out, "Lord, Son of David, have mercy on me! My daughter is suffering terribly from demon-possess" (Matthew 15:22).

Jesus did not say a word to her.

The disciples thought she was bothersome, and they asked

WHAT WAS THE PURPOSE OF HIS COMING?

Him, "Send her away" (verse 23c). Here, my imagination says to me the rain has already begun pouring down.

Jesus told her, "I was sent only to the lost sheep of Israel" (verse 24). Remember, this woman was a Gentile—not an Israelite. Again, my imagination continued with the situation; I envisioned the raging flood waters rapidly reaching up to her neck. What did this woman do in this situation?

The Canaanite woman knelt on her knees before Jesus and pleaded, "Lord, help me!" (verse 25).

Jesus said to her, "It's not right to take the children's bread and toss it to the dogs" (verse 26). The word "children" refers to God's covenant people, the Israelites, and the word "dogs" to the Gentiles.

When the woman heard those words coming out of Jesus' mouth, I imagined, it was as if a terrible tornado had hit her. How much humiliation could she take? Was her heart so troubled by this that it caused her mind and thoughts to wander away from Jesus? Who in the world could withstand this?

This loving mother said, "Yes, Lord, but even the dogs eat the crumbs that fall from their masters' table" (verse 27). This woman humbled herself even more, for she knew that even a crumb (a word) from Jesus was more than sufficient for her daughter to be healed. Her response reveals how strong her faith was in Jesus, the Rock.

Jesus answered, "Woman, you have great faith! Your request is granted. And her daughter was healed from that very hour" (verse 28).

Oh, that we, when going through hard circumstances of any kind, would all demonstrate that same humility, faith, and trust in the Lord? If we do, remember, in due time, the Lord will lift us up! (Please read Matthew 15:21–28 for better understanding.)

Now, about Father Abraham. He took his one and only son, Isaac, to sacrifice him as a burnt offering to God in obedience to His command (please read Genesis 22:1–14). "Abraham took the wood for the burnt offering and placed it on his son Isaac, and he himself carried the fire and the knife."

As they both walked together, Isaac spoke up, "Father?"

Abraham responded, "Yes, my son?"

Isaac asked, "The fire and wood are here, …but where is the lamb for the burnt offering?"

Because of his strong faith, Abraham was able to answer, "God himself will provide the lamb for the burnt offering, my son" (verses 6–8).

Abraham perhaps did not show any emotion whatsoever on his face and did not so much as let his voice crack, for he knew that if he did, Isaac would become suspicious. In fact, he maintained his composure and remained as smooth as butter. Although Abraham loved his son, Isaac, he loved the Lord so much more, for he knew God was faithful, so he was determined to be obedient to His command. Because of his deep faith in the Lord, He provided a ram for the burnt offering and spared Isaac.

Besides the Canaanite woman and Abraham, we find all the prophets, Job, Stephen, one who saw the resurrected Christ standing at the right side of the Father in heaven (Acts 7:55–56), all the disciples (except Judas Iscariot) mentioned in the Scriptures who were perfect examples of those who built their house (faith) upon the Rock. As believers, we must pray that God increases our faith and helps us learn to replace our self-centered life with one that is Christ-centered, dying to self and allowing Christ to live in and through us. Apostle Paul says, "I have been crucified with Christ and I no longer live, but Christ lives in me. The life I live in the body, I live by faith in the Son of God, who loved me and gave himself for me" (Galatians 2:20). Paul's testimony is truly overwhelming, for until his Damascus Road experience (please read Acts 9:1–20), when the Lord Jesus Christ transformed his heart, he was known as Saul, the destroyer of early Christians. He dragged many out of their homes and synagogues, put some in prison, and took part in the stoning deaths of others—namely Stephen, who was full of the Holy Spirit (Acts 7:58–60).

Although we may not have committed any of the same unrighteous acts as Paul did in his early days, can we testify as he did, "I have been crucified with Christ and I no longer live, but Christ lives in me. The life I live in the body, I live by faith in the Son of God, who loved me and gave himself for me"? I know I cannot, for when I compare my faith to his, I'm far, far away.

Jesus traveled back to Nazareth, His hometown, and on the Sabbath day, He went to the synagogue, and the attendant handed Him a scroll, and He stood up to read, giving reverence to the Word of God. As He unrolled it, there was a prophecy written about Himself by Isaiah the prophet,

> *The Spirit of the Sovereign Lord is on me, because the Lord has anointed me to proclaim good news to the poor. He has sent me to bind up the brokenhearted, to proclaim freedom for the captives and release from darkness for the prisoners, to proclaim the year of the Lord's favor.*
>
> **Isaiah 61:1–2a**
> **(Emphasis added by the author)**

This is quoted in Luke 4:18–19.

Then He sat down to teach, for it was the custom during those days for the rabbis to sit down while teaching, and He began to tell them, "Today this scripture is fulfilled in your hearing" (Luke 4:21b). Those who heard Him were in awe at the "gracious words"

(Luke 4:22b) He spoke and wondered how a carpenter's son (unschooled) could speak with such wisdom (please read Luke 4:16–22).

As the Lord continued teaching there on other matters, those same people were so outraged at His message that they became very furious and drove Him out of their town. Instead of feeling tremendously blessed that God Himself came down to serve them in their own synagogue in Nazareth, some of these individuals worked themselves up to the point of wanting to kill Him (please read Luke 4:23–30).

As we continue to read Luke 4:31–37, also Mark 1:21–27, we will notice Jesus always went to the Synagogue on Sabbath day, whatever town He visited, this time in Capernaum. There, He served by teaching the Scriptures and healing and rebuking those oppressed by demons. The people were amazed at His authoritative teachings, the power, and authority over the evil spirit. He set the example for the world, as followers of Jesus Christ; we too should make every effort to attend church services regularly. We should worship the Lord and serve in any capacity we can to be a blessing to others. God will surely reward us in a mighty way!

It appears Jesus always kept busy. Upon leaving the synagogue (please read Mark 1:29–34; Luke 4:38–41), He went to the home of Simon and Andrew (the disciples), where Jesus was immediately told that Simon Peter's mother-in-law was ill and weak with a fever. He went straight in and held her and helped her to get up, and instantly, the fever left her. On that very same day in the evening, after sunset, to keep up the Sabbath's law, many people brought those who were ill and suffering from various diseases, as well as some who had evil spirits. He healed the sick and drove out the demons from those who were possessed.

Although Jesus was constantly busy preaching, teaching, and healing the sick, He was found the very next morning, "while it was still dark," out in "a solitary place, where he prayed" (Mark 1:35). Wouldn't it be wonderful if every Christian would adopt that same routine? No matter how hectic your day might have been, just imagine starting the next day, or every day, while it's still dark, in a quiet, peaceful place, praying and praising the Lord. What a blessing it would be to have such intimacy with God!

In Mark 2:14–17, we read of a large crowd meeting in the home of Matthew, also known as Levi, the apostle, who was a tax collector. In those days, this segment of society was considered to be full of swindlers, for they often collected more money than the law required and filled up their pockets, making themselves rich. Matthew had called this meeting; he wanted his friends, colleagues, and others to hear what Jesus, the teacher, had to say. The Pharisees were one of the five sects of Jews. They considered themselves to be "righteous," meaning they were, in actuality, self-righteous. They had been following Jesus from place to place, trying to keep up with what He was doing and saying. When they noticed where Jesus was having dinner, they made a comment, "Why does he eat with tax collectors and 'sinners'?" (Mark 2:16).

Jesus responded to them, "It is not the healthy who need a doctor, but the sick. *I have not come to call the righteous, but sinners*" (verse 17) (emphasis added by the author).

In those days, the tax collectors did what they were not supposed to do. How about today? Does anyone take bribes, or does everyone pay their taxes?

As I was writing this, I thought of the self-righteous Pharisees, and a message came to my heart: don't we all try to justify our actions at some time or another? For example, I have heard with my own ears people say, "I don't sin; I've never killed anybody; I don't steal; or I don't cheat on my spouse." And some say, "I haven't committed any major sins." My dear readers, I must say that there is no such thing as a major or minor sin. God doesn't classify sin, for all sin separates us from Him. Saint Paul said, "For all have sinned and fall short of the glory of God" (Romans 3:23). We could search the wide world over and probably not find anyone who's never told a lie. A lie is anything that's untrue, and it can be a word or a deed. Jesus taught us, "God is spirit, and his worshipers must worship in spirit and in truth" (John 4:24).

All these years, it was my understanding that God does not classify sin as minor or major until this morning, September 27, 2018. As I asked the Lord for my daily word, I opened the Bible, and it was John chapter nineteen, and the Lord opened my spiritual eyes when I read verse eleven. The situation was, during the interrogation by Pilate, Jesus responded to his questioning, "Therefore the one who handed me over to you is guilty of a *greater sin*" (John 19:11b) (emphasis added by the author). As I was digesting this, the Lord put broader thoughts in my heart. During the Last Supper, Jesus spoke about Judas Iscariot, His betrayer, "But woe to that man who betrays the Son of Man! It would be better for him if he had not been born" (Matthew 26:24). A gravest sin, for he betrayed not a mere man, but the Son of God.

The last thing the Lord put in my heart was not all sins are forgiven; Jesus said, "I tell you the truth, all the sins and blasphemies of men will be forgiven them. But whoever blasphemies against the Holy Spirit will never be forgiven; he is guilty of an eternal sin" (Mark 3:28–29). Now I know that God does classify the sins. So be aware!

The name "Jesus" means, "He will save his people from their sins" (Matthew 1:21). What does God consider sin? Not only disobeying the ten commandments that were given to Moses in the Old Testament but much more. When we take it upon ourselves to do the opposite of anything that God tells us to do or not to do, this is considered a sin. Jesus Christ came not only to sacrifice His life for our salvation but also to teach us how to live the righteous life that God the Father expected from His children. This is why it is vitally important that we study the Word of God, specifically the teachings of Jesus Christ, which can be found in all four Gospels: Matthew, Mark, Luke, and John.

Let me just quote what Jesus said regarding what makes a man unclean or unrighteous,

> *What comes out of a man, that defiles a man. For from within, out of the heart of men, proceed evil thoughts, adulteries, fornications, murders, thefts, covetousness, wickedness, deceit, lewdness, an evil eye, blasphemy, pride, foolishness. All these evil things come from within and defile a man.*
>
> **Mark 7:20–23 (NKJV)**
> **(Emphasis added by the author)**

I urge you, my readers, to please pick up your Bible and study the Word of God; the more of His words we have within us, the less room there will be for evil thoughts to get into our hearts. Practice it, for practice makes us perfect, and it will become our natural response. If we don't study His words and apply them to our lives, how can we call ourselves Christians, followers of Jesus Christ?

Many of us tend to blame Adam and Eve for bringing sin into the world by disobeying God's one and only commandment; when we can't seem to have the desire or self-discipline to obey the two that Jesus gave us. He summed everything up with this,

> *'Love the Lord your God with all your heart and with all your soul and with all your mind.' This is the first and greatest commandment. And the second is like it: 'Love your neighbor as yourself.' All the Law and the Prophets hang on these two commandments.*
>
> **Matthew 22:37–40**
> **(Emphasis added by the author)**

This is an easy way to remember how to put the second commandment into practice, for this is the golden rule! Jesus said, "So in everything [in every situation], do to others what you would have them do to you [when you are in their shoes], for this sums up the Law and the Prophets" (Matthew 7:12). God is love, and He demonstrated His love towards us by sending His one and only Son and gave us eternal life. Therefore, in return, aren't we obligated to obey Him? So, let's love our God with all our heart, mind, and soul and show His love in us toward our fellow human beings. (Please read 1 John 4:7–21 for better understanding.)

Love is not just a word that we say to someone, "I love you." It's much more than that; it's an action. Apostle Paul explains the meaning of the word "love" like this,

> *Love is patient, love is kind. It does not envy, it does not boast, it is not proud. It is not rude, it is not self-seeking, it is not easily angered, it keeps no record of wrongs. Love does not delight in evil but rejoices with the truth. It always protects, always trusts, always hopes, always perseveres.*
>
> **1 Corinthians 13:4–7**
> **(Emphasis added by the author)**

(Please read 1 Corinthians 13:4–13 for a greater understanding.)

Who do you consider as your neighbor? It's not only just the people next door to your apartment or house but whoever sits next to you while using public transportation such as buses, trains, airplanes, or luxury boats/ships. Or it could be someone sitting next to you in a sports arena. Furthermore, while you are walking in the street and find someone who is on a footpath needing help, he/she is your neighbor, and that's where your act of love/kindness takes place. A stranger helping the stranger, beyond our wild imagination, is depicted in Luke 10:25–35 (please read), and Jesus commands us, "Go and do likewise" (Luke 10:37). For this is true love toward a neighbor!

God created man and woman, not man and man or woman and woman; however, these days, marrying the same sex has become a social lifestyle. Jesus taught us there was a reason for the Creator to create both sexes, "Therefore a man shall leave his father and mother and be joined to his wife, and they shall become one flesh" (Genesis 2:24, NKJV). Therefore, any other way is not acceptable. God promised Abraham that his descendants would be as numerous as the sands on the seashore and that He would make of him a father of many nations. If it had been nations of homosexuals, would we even be here? Would God's promises have been fulfilled, or would God be made out to be a liar? Can homosexuals produce children? Will they inherit the kingdom of God?

Let's read what Apostle Paul specifically wrote about this matter and many other ungodly characters,

> *Do you not know that the wicked will not inherit the kingdom of God? Do not be deceived: Neither the sexually immoral nor idolaters nor adulterers nor male prostitutes nor homosexual nor thieves nor the greedy nor drunkards nor slanderers nor swindlers will inherit the kingdom of God.*
>
> **1 Corinthians 6:9–10**
> **(Emphasis added by the author)**

But He continued to write with great hope of encouragement, "And that is what some of you were. But you were washed, you were sanctified, you were justified in the name of the Lord Jesus Christ and by the Spirit of our God" (verse 11). That means you, too, can be blessed as some of them were in his time!

I know of one lesbian couple that accepted Jesus as their Savior and Lord, and God has been using them in a mighty way. They began working in the community and have already saved many souls; one of them even has the spiritual gift of prophesying. Oh, what a blessing it is to watch them grow spiritually! God is full of love; there is no love that can be compared to His agape (unconditional love). Psalmist said, *"When my father and my mother forsake me, Then the LORD will take care of me"* (Psalm 27:10, NKJV) (emphasis added by the author). The whole world might hate you, but you can rest assured that God will never. I beseech you, my dear, not to follow the world; our Lord is very compassionate, and He doesn't want any soul to perish. He is waiting on you patiently; turn your heart toward Him in repentance and receive Jesus as your Lord and Savior; you will have eternal/everlasting life.

Please read Romans 1:18 through the end of the chapter and pay attention to verses 26 and 27. If you would kindly read Genesis 18:20–19:29, you will learn why God destroyed Sodom and Gomorrah, the two cities, from the face of the earth by fire because those cities were polluted by homosexuality. The Lord said, "The outcry against Sodom and Gomorrah is so great and their sin so grievous" (Genesis 18:20).

In today's world, divorce has become like a fashion trend: if it doesn't suit you, remove it and try another marriage. Some people continue "trying on" new marriages over and over again for years, and the more divorces, the more popular the person seems to become. In my country growing up, I never heard of divorce in the 1950s, '60s, or even in the '70s, but now it is spreading like wildfire.

Let us see what Jesus had to say about this subject when the Pharisees asked,

> *"Is it lawful for a man to divorce his wife for any and every reason?" "Haven't you read," he replied,*

WHAT WAS THE PURPOSE OF HIS COMING?

> *"that at the beginning the Creator 'made them male and female,' and said, 'For this reason a man will leave his father and mother and be united to his wife, and the two will become one flesh'? So they are no longer two, but one. Therefore what God has joined together, let man not separate."*
>
> **Matthew 19:3–6**
> **(Emphasis added by the author)**

What a strong warning! Are we Christians obeying Him?

As the Pharisees continued to question Him, Jesus told them no divorce is acceptable except for one reason, which is *"fornication."* There are consequences if the divorcee chooses to marry someone else, "And I [Jesus] say to you, whoever divorces his wife, except for sexual immorality, and marries another, commits adultery; and whoever marries her who is divorced commits adultery" (Matthew 19:9, NKJV). So, before you think of divorce, always remember that your marriage was a sacred sacrament, a vow, in the presence of God; He witnessed it. God instituted the oneness of man and woman, meaning they would become one flesh and produce godly children. God hates divorce (please read Malachi 2:14–16).

My friend, you may not have stabbed anyone with a knife or shot them with a gun, but you may have committed murder with your tongue. The tongue may be a small part of the body, yet it is the most powerful weapon for its size. The same tongue can be used to bless God or to curse our fellow man, encourage or discourage, uplift or depress, build up or destroy; in fact, people can actually use their tongue to provoke another person to murder or suicide, "But no man can tame the tongue. It is an unruly evil, full of deadly poison. With it we bless our God and Father, and with it we curse men, who have been made in the similitude of God" (James 3:8–9, NKJV).

Most people don't even realize that boasting is a sin because they lack the wisdom to acknowledge the fact that God gave them everything they have; many of them were literally brought from rags to riches. King David, a man after God's own heart, said to the Lord in prayers, "Everything comes from you, and we have given you only what comes from your hand" (1 Chronicles 29:14). I wish everyone would learn this lesson and act upon it. God hates a proud heart and a lying tongue (Proverbs 6:16–17).

The tongue can have a devastating effect on a whole family or even an entire community. At times, it may begin with a tongue used to entice an innocent young child or even an adult into destroying their lives through the use of drugs, alcohol, or even prostitution, pornography, and other wicked schemes. Sadly, greed and the lust for money are usually the motivations behind such actions. Jesus taught us one cannot serve God and Mammon (money, the devil) at the same time (Matthew 6:24).

If God lights a spark, who are we to put it out? Who has the audacity to stop something God Almighty has started? A woman does—when she has an abortion. An abortion, whether it's done at the moment of conception or any time throughout the pregnancy, is murder; thus, it is a sin in the eyes of God. Thousands of years ago, King David wrote, "For you created my inmost being; you knit me together in my mother's womb. I praise you because I am fearfully and wonderfully made; your works are wonderful, I know that full well" (Psalm 139:13–14).

Now let us go to the book of Jeremiah, where God Himself said to this prophet, "Before I formed you in the womb I knew you, before you were born I set you apart; I appointed you as a prophet to the nations" (Jeremiah 1:5).

When a person chooses to abort a baby, she usually gives no thought to the tremendous blessing that individual might have been to the world and unto God. It never enters her mind that she's putting an end to a future before it had an opportunity to begin.

WHAT WAS THE PURPOSE OF HIS COMING?

No one knows what blessings God's plan held for the future of that unborn child. People who think that abortion is not a crime against God are disobeying Him due to their ignorance, for God commanded us, "You shall not murder" (Exodus 20:13). Take it to heart; the Word of God says, "Sons are a heritage from the LORD, children a reward from him" (Psalm 127:3). My advice to you is, if you cannot take care of the child, give him/her up for adoption, because there are many couples wanting to have children but are not able to, so your child will be a blessing for them as well as to the child itself. Don't be a murderer, please, for God records every deed, good and bad, in the Book of Life, which He will open on judgment day and reward us according to our deeds (please read Revelation 20:12–14).

The King of all kings worked relentlessly and traveled continuously at a time when there were no automobiles, motorbikes, or bicycles; in fact, most likely, His mode of transportation would have been either His feet or a fisherman's boat. He traveled from Galilee to Jerusalem, stopping through villages and towns, teaching and preaching the good news of the kingdom of God, healing every kind of illness, raising the dead, and doing miraculous signs and wonders.

During His ministry, Jesus often taught in parables, which are earthly stories with heavenly meanings. Jesus knew what is in heaven, for He came down from there, and we people know only what is on the earth. So, by comparing the earthly events to the heavenly ones, He gave us a better understanding of His message and fulfilled another prophecy, "I will open my mouth in parable; I will utter hidden things, things from of old" (Psalm 78:2). This is quoted in Matthew 13:35.

Let's look at the content of the two parables and see what effect they have on us as we read. In the first one, Jesus said,

> *Or suppose a woman has ten silver coins and loses*

one. Does she not light a lamp, sweep the house and search carefully until she finds it? And when she finds it, she calls her friends and neighbors together and says, 'Rejoice with me; I have found my lost coin.' In the same way, I tell you, there is rejoicing in the presence of the angels of God over one sinner who repents.

**Luke 15:8–10
(Emphasis added by the author)**

Now, let's look at another parable, a perfect illustration of how people respond in different ways to any given situation, depending on their nature. In Luke 15:11 through its entirety, Jesus told a story about a man and his two sons. The youngest was a little wild, and he decided to ask his father to give him half of his inheritance so that he could go out and live independently as he desired. When his father gave him the money, he headed out to a faraway country to enjoy his life. Once there, he lavishly spent his fortune in the bad company of friends and "with prostitutes" (verse 30). When all his money was gone, he suddenly realized that all of his so-called friends were gone as well.

Then came a severe famine in that land, and the young man couldn't find anyone to give him so much as a morsel of food. He decided to get a job there, at least as a servant. When he was hired, his master sent him to feed his pigs. The young man was so hungry that he eagerly desired to eat some of the food that he was feeding the pigs. When his thoughts, mind, and heart came to reality, he said to himself, I better return home and be my father's servant, for his hired help ate lavishly while I am dying of starvation here (verses 17–18a). And he decided to tell his father, "I have sinned against heaven and against you. I am no longer worthy to be called your son; make me like one of your hired men" (Luke 15:18b–19).

And the young man set out on his journey right away; when the father saw his son coming from a very long distance, he had compassion and ran and hugged his son and kissed him. After hearing what his son had to say, the father called his servants and told them to dress him in his finest attire and to prepare for a lavish celebration. This is exactly how our compassionate and loving God the Father treats His children when they repent of their sins and come to Him.

Meanwhile, the older son was working in the field, and when he heard all the commotion, he asked his servant what was going on. The servant told him that his father was celebrating his brother's return. Upon hearing the news, the older brother became outraged, for he felt that he had remained faithful and obedient to his father, and yet he was never recognized or acknowledged, and he refused to enter the house. The father went out and pleaded with him to come celebrate his brother—who had been lost but was now found, and who had been dead, meaning spiritually dead or separated from God due to his sins, but was now alive, for he repented his sins.

Now, let us compare the above with our practical life. Suppose you have five children. One of them, for some unknown reason, runs away from home; you immediately contact the police and the media and do a web search, hoping the child will come home or at least contact you. Your thoughts are more preoccupied with the child who is missing due to the fact that his or her safety and security are in question, or their very life could be in jeopardy.

Try to imagine the relief a parent feels when they get that long-awaited phone call. I can visualize the tears of joy streaming down their cheeks at the sound of their child's voice saying, "Mom and Dad, I'm so sorry. May I please come back home?" I can sense the unimaginable feelings they have once they're holding that child in their arms. At a time like that, parents, siblings, extended family, friends, and neighbors must feel sheer elation.

Although we love all of our children equally, it is impossible not to have special feelings for that child who was lost and then found, for it's as if he or she was dead and then was brought back to life. It's impossible to conceive of the celebration our heavenly Father and all of His angels have in heaven when one of His lost children repent of their sins and returns to Him from their rebellious ways.

Jesus said in Matthew 9:12–13 that He came to bring the sinners unto Him for their spiritual healing, just as a doctor would invite the sick people to treat their physical or mental illnesses. Indeed, Jesus came for the sinners; the proof of an awesome illustration is found in John 4:4–43. A Samaritan woman, who had been married five times, yet the man she was living with was not her husband, verses 16–18, now had an encounter with a stranger.

Jesus was headed toward Galilee from Judea. He went through Samaria, verses 3–4, a place usually not entered by Jews in order to avoid contact with the mixed race. This race consisted of the Jews who had married the Assyrians, and they were considered low class.

When Jesus arrived in a town called Sychar, the woman also went there to fetch water from a well, but instead, Jesus offered her living water and said,

> *Everyone who drinks this water [well water] will be thirsty again, but whoever drinks the water I give him will never thirst. Indeed, the water I give him will become in him a spring of water welling up to eternal life.*
>
> **John 4:13–14**
> **(Emphasis added by the author)**

The woman became very interested in the water this stranger was offering, for perhaps it would make life easier for her; maybe she would no longer have to carry water from the well.... But Jesus was referring to the Holy Spirit (please read John 7:37–39 for clear understanding).

Since the woman was so eager to receive the water from Him, the stranger told her, first, go and bring her husband. The woman honestly told Him she had no husband. But Jesus/stranger convicted her of her sinful lifestyle by telling her she had had five husbands and the one who was currently living with her was not her husband. We can see this woman was immediately fed spiritually, for she was able to recognize this was no ordinary Jewish man but a prophet, verses 16–19.

The climax of this lengthy, unexpected, unprepared, most exciting debate of all times is verse 26, and its powerful effects are in verses 39–42.

Upon hearing the woman's statement, "'I know that Messiah' (called Christ) 'is coming. When he comes, he will explain everything to us'" (verse 25).

Jesus declared/confirmed to this sinful woman, "I who speak to you am he" (verse 26). Dear friend, here I ask you to take a moment to visualize yourself in this woman's place; try to imagine the joy and excitement she felt when the stranger revealed Himself to her (face to face) by saying, "I who speak to you am he." Your awaited Messiah, the Christ, is speaking to you!

As I was studying this above verse, I found myself empowered by the Holy Spirit to write the entire event in this book. It was a powerful, overwhelming experience for me! So much so that it seemed as if I had the same feelings she must have had when Jesus Christ, whom she had been waiting for, God in the human flesh, stood in front of her and revealed Himself, saying, "I who speak to you am he"!

The Samaritan woman instantly believed in Jesus. This became the turning point in her life. She left the water jar and ran home to testify to the people of the city what she had seen and heard.

Because of her testimony, many Samaritans believed in Jesus, thus resulting in them proclaiming, "This man really is the Savior of the world" (end of verse 42). Likewise, if each one of us had her enthusiasm, and if we would be willing to allow God the Father to use us to lead others to His Son, soon the whole world would be saved.

Years after I wrote this, I served in one of the prisons in Florida. It was a habit; each time I went to the prison, I would ask Jesus, "What shall I speak to Your children, my Lord?" This time, God put the thought in my heart to speak about the Samaritan woman. As I explained to some of the residents there how Jesus used a woman who had had five husbands to serve Him, one of the young women very enthusiastically asked me, "Where is it? Where is it written in the Bible?" In her heart, she knew there was hope!

I'm sure there are many like her in this world. My dear friend, yes, there is hope. Jesus came to save the sinners like you and me because He loves us unconditionally. Whatever fallen state you may be in, speak to Him, invite Him into your heart, and allow Him to shape you into the person He created and designed you to be!

Jesus Christ came to give us peace. About five hundred years before His birth, the prophet Zechariah prophesied and recorded in his book, "He will proclaim peace to the nations" (9:10d). Jesus is our peace, as prophesied by prophet Micah, "And he will be their peace" (Micah 5:5a). Jesus said, "I leave you peace; my peace I give you. I do not give it to you as the world does. So don't let your hearts be troubled or afraid" (John 14:27, NCV). Apostle Paul wrote, "But now in Christ Jesus, you who were far away from God are brought near through the blood of Christ's death. *Christ himself is our peace*" (Ephesians 2:13–14a, NCV) (emphasis added by the author). Isaiah prophesied that one of His names would be "Prince of Peace" (Isaiah 9:6, NCV).

Jesus came to give us the biggest gift: the Holy Spirit! John the Baptist foretold that Jesus' baptism would be much greater than his,

> *I baptize you with water to show that your hearts and lives have changed. But there is one coming after me who is greater than I am, whose sandals I am not good enough to carry. He will baptize you with the Holy Spirit and fire.*
>
> **Matthew 3:11 (NCV)**
> **(Emphasis added by the author)**

And regarding the Holy Spirit, Jesus made promises to His disciples at various times (please read John 14:16–17, 26; 15:26; 16:7–8, 13–15) that after He departed from them, He would ask the Father to send the Counselor, the Holy Spirit, to be with them forever. Not only with them but also will be with all the believers who receive Jesus as their Savior and baptize in the name of the Father, Son, and the Holy Spirit.

Surely, the Lord kept His promise. Ten days after Jesus went back to heaven, where He was glorified by His Father, suddenly, like the sound of a violent wind (Holy Spirit), came down from heaven and filled the house where the apostles and others were staying, one hundred twenty in all. The disciples were empowered by the Holy Spirit, who came to rest upon them in what appeared to be split tongues of fire. As a result, they were enabled to speak in different languages which they never knew or spoke before (please read Acts 2:1–4, 11). The Jews from all over the world (please read Acts 2:5–13) were gathered in Jerusalem during this time to celebrate the feast of Pentecost, also known as the feast of the first fruits of the Harvest, and they were amazed, for all of them heard the message from the disciples in their own native language. But some of them thought apostles were drunk.

In the Old Testament time, the Holy Spirit was given only to certain people whom God chose and anointed them to be judges and kings. For example, Judge Othniel (Judges 3:10); King Saul (1 Samuel 10:1, 6, 10); and King David (1 Samuel 16:13). But now, the Holy Spirit indwells in every believer, as mentioned in the previous paragraph. He convicts us of our sins, guides us to the right path, and comforts us in our distress. Many times a day, I pray to the Father in heaven to fill me with the Holy Spirit and take away evil from me. I hope and pray that you, too, will make a similar request to the Father.

In the latter part of writing this book, I went back and read the above portion again and did more studies on John, chapters fourteen through seventeen, and then God revealed to me greater things. Jesus said, "But the Helper will teach you everything and will cause you to remember all that I told you. This Helper is the Holy Spirit whom the Father will send in my name" (John 14:26, NCV). As the Holy Spirit gives us an understanding of Jesus' teachings, and if we obey them, there is a greater reward which our Lord Himself promised, "If people love me, they will obey my teaching. My Father will love them, and *we* will come to them and make *our* home with them" (John 14:23, NCV) (emphasis added by the author). What an awesome promise! I must say this: the Bible still is like an ocean to me. After all these years of Bible studies, this is the day (November 23, 2015) the Lord opened my spiritual eyes and gave me the understanding of His promise and the use of plural forms "we" and "our" (the Trinity). Jesus again used "we," the plural form in John 17:11, "us" in verse 21, and another "we" in verse 22 of the same chapter. Up until today, I knew God used the plural forms only in the book of Genesis during the creation of human beings. At this, I exclaimed, "How great Thou art to reveal these marvelous things to me, the least of the least!

My beloved readers, do not look for God far away; He will be with you and inside of you if you would study Jesus' teachings

WHAT WAS THE PURPOSE OF HIS COMING?

and obey them. Honor the Lord with all your heart and revere His words, for He came down from the highest position to give you what the world cannot give.

Jesus came to establish His church on this earth; when Jesus and His disciples were together in the region of Caesarea Philippi, He asked them if they knew who He was. Peter responded, "You are the Christ, the Son of the living God" (Matthew 16:16). As their conversation continued, Jesus said to Simon Peter, verses 17–19, but I would quote only 17 and 18a (NCV), "You are blessed, Simon son of Jonah, because no person taught you that. My Father in heaven showed you who I am. So I tell you, you are Peter. On this rock I will build my church." "Rock" means Jesus Himself. (For better understanding, please read Matthew 16:14–19). If we read the book of Acts, we notice the establishment of the first church in Jerusalem and its expansion to the surrounding areas and other countries.

Apostle Paul gives us a clear understanding of the foundation of the church,

> *Consequently, you are no longer foreigners and aliens, but fellow citizens with God's people, and members of God's household, built on the foundation of the apostles and prophets, with Christ Jesus himself as the chief cornerstone.*
>
> **Ephesians 2:19–20**
> **(Emphasis added by the author)**

"Church" means believers, the body of Christ (1 Corinthians 12:27–28), gathered, where they would worship and praise the Lord, preach the good news, thus build up their faith completely in Jesus Christ, and strengthen each other spiritually. They would also partake in the holy communion (breaking of the bread) on Sundays (Acts 20:7), proclaiming Jesus' death until He returns (1 Corinthians 11:24–27). There were no church buildings during the apostles' time like we have today. It seems like, most of the time, they gathered in someone's house (Romans 16:3–5; 1 Corinthians 16:19; Philemon 2).

Jesus taught various subjects throughout the Gospels. I couldn't cover them all, so I beg you to read and then study them; begin with the Sermon on the Mount, recorded in Matthew chapters 5–7. As you study them, I pray: may the Lord transform your heart to practice them in your daily life, and may you receive showers of blessings.

THE OBEDIENT SON

Jesus related the purpose of His coming in many different places in the Scriptures, and yet He never took credit for Himself. Although Jesus was a King, and under normal circumstances, kings are the ones who are being served; instead, Jesus the King said, "In the same way, the Son of Man did not come to be served. He came to serve others and to give his life as a ransom for many people" (Mark 10:45, NCV). (For better understanding, please read Mark 10:42–45.) If our precious Savior, the King of all kings, could humble Himself, become a servant, and in every way set a perfect example for us, then surely, we must strive to do no less.

Jesus came into this world to give us the message from God the Father, just as God had revealed it to Moses, "So I will give them a prophet like you, who is one of their own people [Israelite]. I will tell him what to say, and he will tell them everything I command" (Deuteronomy 18:18, NCV). The confirmation of this can be seen in the last Gospel, where Jesus said,

> *The things I taught were not from myself. The Father who sent me told me what to say and what to teach. And I know that eternal life comes from what the Father commands. So whatever I say is what the Father*

told me to say.

John 12:49–50 (NCV)
(Emphasis added by the author)

Please do not take it too lightly; instead, make it a number one priority in your life to study the Word of God and put it into practice—just as God the Father commanded the three disciples during Jesus' transfiguration, "This is my Son, whom I have chosen. Listen to him!" (Luke 9:35, NCV). God declared to Moses the consequences of disobeying His words, "This prophet will speak for me; anyone who does not listen when he speaks will answer to me" (Deuteronomy 18:19, NCV).

If anyone chooses to ignore Jesus' teachings, the Father already has a judgment planned. And Jesus confirms it, "There is a judge for those who refuse to believe in me and do not accept my words. The word I have taught will be their judge on the last day [on judgment day]" (John 12:48, NCV). Apostle Paul explains, "Then he will punish those who do not know God and who do not obey the Good News about our Lord Jesus Christ" (2 Thessalonians 1:8, NCV). (For better understanding, please read verses 6–8.)

The purpose of His coming is continued in the following chapters: "The Fulfillment of the Prophecies Regarding Jesus' Suffering," "The Crucifixion," and "The Resurrection."

CHAPTER 6:

THE LIGHT IN THE MIDST OF THE DARKNESS

Jesus said, "I am the light of the world. The person who follows me will never live in darkness but will have the light that gives life" (John 8:12, NCV).

On July 16, 2009, I happened to be watching *The Oprah Winfrey Show*. That day, she had two guests on her show, and both were women who had been convicted of murder. One of these women shot and killed her husband, and the other shot and killed her father, and yet both shootings had been in self-defense.

The woman who killed her father had done so in response to the despicable acts he had committed against her, beginning at the age of nine and continuing throughout her teenage years until she moved out of the house. She found out later that her younger sister had been going through the very same situation; thus, in a fit of uncontrollable rage, she shot and killed her father. Her lack of self-control at that moment, at the age of eighteen, resulted in eighteen years of incarceration.

That afternoon, as she sat on the stage next to Oprah, I thought to myself, *This thirty-six-year-old woman certainly doesn't look like a person who just got out of prison.* No, instead, she looked as if she might have just returned from an extended luxury cruise, for her face, full of joy and peace, was as bright as the sun. After listening to her conversation, I understood why she had that special aura, for she had repented of her sins and asked the Lord for forgiveness, not only for herself but for her father, the enemy, as well.

Jesus taught us how to pray, "Forgive us for our sins, just as we have forgiven those who sinned against us" (Matthew 6:12, NCV). As He continues, "Yes, if you forgive others for their sins, your Father in heaven will also forgive you for your sins. *But if you don't forgive others, your Father in heaven will not forgive your sins*" (verses 14–15, NCV) (emphasis added by the author). It shows how important it is to forgive others for our salvation. If you are unable to approach the person, you can always pray for him or her as Jesus instructed us, "Bless those who curse you, pray for those who are cruel to you" (Luke 6:28, NCV).

The Word of God says, "The effective, fervent prayer of a righteous man avails much" (James 5:16, NKJV). And that's a promise, assuring us that our earnest prayers will always receive an answer. In fact, when God the Father says they "avails much," it means they are powerful not because of who we are but because of the One who answers the prayer.

Years after I wrote the above, a thought came into my heart, saying, "How amazing our God is; millions of people from all over the world, day and night, must be praying and crying out to Him at the same time, and He hears them all. Whereas, as a human being, if two people would speak to me at a time, I would tell them, 'Stop, one at a time, please,' for I couldn't understand a word they were saying. What an amazing power of God!"

The act of repentance is important to believers, for it involves the changing of the person's heart, mind, and attitude toward his or her sin. In order to have a right relationship with the Lord, we must

THE LIGHT IN THE MIDST OF THE DARKNESS

confess our sins. We notice an example: Apostle Paul commented on the repentance of the Corinthians and its result,

> *Now I am happy, not because you were made sad, but because your sorrow made you change your lives. You became sad in the way God wanted you to, so you were not hurt by us in any way. The kind of sorrow God wants makes people change their hearts and lives. This leads to salvation, and you cannot be sorry for that. But the kind of sorrow world has brings death [spiritual death].*
>
> **2 Corinthians 7:9–10 (NCV)**
> **(Emphasis added by the author)**

Godly sorrow takes place in a person's heart as a result of the Holy Spirit convicting (reminding) them of sin (John 16:8). This dear lady was a perfect example of why Jesus came into this world. He brought the light, where before there had been only darkness, as Jesus said in John 8:12, which is quoted at the beginning of this chapter. This young lady probably grew up in complete darkness with no exposure to the Scriptures in her home, but God was with her. The Lord took her incarceration, which the world normally considers a curse or shame, and turned it into a great blessing. There, she had the hunger and thirst to study the Scriptures, so she spent her time wisely, reading the whole Bible several times. The Word of God is so powerful and much needed in our daily life for our spiritual strength to keep us from falling; we read,

> *God's word is alive and working and is sharper than a double-edged sword. It cuts all the way into us, where the soul and the spirit are joined, to the center of our joints and bones. And it judges the thoughts and feelings in our hearts.*
>
> **Hebrews 4:12 (NCV)**
> **(Emphasis added by the author)**

JESUS, THE KING OF KINGS

In the Holy Bible, the word "darkness" usually refers to our sinful nature, our being lost, or the evil within us—but just as Jesus washed away this woman's sins and made her as white as snow, He will do the same for anyone who is remorseful of their rebellious (unrighteous) acts, and welcomes Jesus into their hearts as their personal Savior; because only God has the ability to both forgive and forget all our sins.

I pray that the Lord will not only bless her abundantly but also bless the feet of those who brought her the good news. Hallelujah! Praise the Lord!

Now, Oprah Winfrey, you have invited millions of guests and audiences to your show, and billions are watching all over the world. You are so brilliant; I still remember when you introduced the young Senator Barack Obama to the world as a presidential candidate, and how it influenced millions of people, especially the women, to vote for him; thus, you made him the president of the United States of America. I can assure you, Oprah, with such ability, you could save many souls and turn the hearts and minds of many men and women to God. All those saved will spend their eternity in heaven, and you will receive a crown of victory when you get there. As Saint Paul wrote,

> *Now, a crown is being held for me—a crown for being right with God. The Lord, the judge who judges rightly, will give the crown to me on that day—not only to me but to all those who have waited with love for him to come again.*
>
> **2 Timothy 4:8 (NCV)**
> **(Emphasis added by the author)**

I pray that God will use you in a mighty way, Oprah.

One would never comprehend how, when, where, or in which direction the Lord will lead and guide a person to mold and prepare the heart of whom He chooses to serve Him. In my case, it was a long process that took at least nine years to manifest in me. If it weren't for the Lord, I do not believe I would have watched the above-mentioned show so intensely in 2009 and written it down. Later in my life, I began to realize that this was the way God began to mold and prepare my heart to do what He wanted me to do. A year later, on Thursday, August 19, 2010, approximately an hour after the daily 5 a.m. teleconference prayer time with Lee Robbins, the pastor of the Kingdom Life Church, my writer Carolyn, Lemma, and other sisters in Christ, I suddenly had an amazing supernatural experience.

Pastor Lee said, "Sister Leela, the Spirit of the Lord says that He hears your deepest cry and that He knows, feels, and understands your desire for you and your husband to walk in faith together and be closer to the Lord. He also told me to let you know that He had been waiting, waiting, and waiting on you. Now is the time to move on—do not put it off! The Holy Spirit will show you what the Lord wants you to do. He will give you understanding where understanding is needed. Do not simply read the Word, but make it personal and devotional. This is your time, and this is your season!"

I met Pastor Lee at Carolyn's house only a couple of months prior to this blessed occasion. He knew nothing about me or my husband's personal or spiritual life except that I was writing a book with the help of one of his church members, Carolyn May. Well, I must say this: when it comes to spirituality, my husband is neither cold nor hot; he is just lukewarm—like Jesus spoke of the church in Laodicea, Revelation 3:16. So, I knew immediately that the message was coming from God, and I revered everything as the pastor spoke by the power of the Holy Spirit.

The following morning, after our routine prayer, as I picked up my Holy Bible, I asked the Lord to show me what He wanted me to do; immediately, the Word of God opened to Isaiah 42. I read the entire chapter, but verses six and seven were the messages that Holy Spirit impressed upon my heart the most. God said,

> *I, the LORD, called you to do right, and I will hold*

> *your hand and protect you. You will be the sign of my agreement with the people, a light to shine for all people. You will help the blind to see. You will free those who are in prison, and you will lead those who live in darkness out of their prison.*
>
> **Isaiah 42:6–7 (NCV)**
> **(Emphasis added by the author)**

In fact, these are the verses that led me to read Isaiah 61:1, which says,

> *The Lord GOD has put his Spirit in me, because the LORD has appointed me to tell the good news to the poor. He has sent me to comfort those whose hearts are broken, to tell the captives they are free, and to tell the prisoners they are released.*
>
> **Isaiah 61:1 (NCV)**
> **(Emphasis added by the author)**

When I read this, it struck my heart, for during all these years, I had thought this was for Jesus to do, not for anyone else. When I talked to the pastor the following day, I told him about the Scriptures the Lord has laid on my heart, and he immediately told me, "Those are the same verses that I was also given, and it means 'ministry.'"

I had no idea it was God who put the desire in my heart to go to the prison in 2001 when I was working in New York. One of my colleagues, Belinda, told me she went to the prison and ministered to the prisoners, but I had never heard of prison ministry, so I do not know where I got the idea to ask her, "Could you also take me to the prison?"

She replied, "It is impossible for you to get into a prison without being on the visitor list, and it is very hard to get on it." So, I left it at that. However, as I was studying the Scriptures, it touched my heart when I came across the words spoken by Jesus in Matthew 25:34–40 (please read for better understanding). I will quote only a portion of verse forty—on judgment day Jesus, the King would tell us, "Anything you did for even the least of my people here, you also did for me" (NCV). And I examined within, and said to myself, I had been doing (unknowingly) all that He said in verses thirty-five and thirty-six, except one thing, which is the last part of verse 36 (NCV), "I was in prison, and you visited me." I got frightened when I read the King of kings in heaven saying to those who did not serve the least of the least, verse 41 (NKJV), "Depart from Me, you cursed, into the everlasting fire prepared for the devil and his angels." I strongly felt that I must serve in prison.

In 2010, as my writer Carolyn and I had gotten to know each other a little better, she told me about her prison services with the Bill Glass Champions for Life Ministry over the last twenty years or so, and I told her about my unfulfilled desire to minister to prisoners. She promised that she would help me.

Pastor Lee had no idea that Carolyn and I had already done the paperwork together and had been registered with the Bill Glass Champions for Life Ministry for the upcoming prison event scheduled on October 9, 2010. It was on this same day that, for the first time, our church was hosting the Women's Annual Conference. Ladies would come from all over the southwest and southeast regions of America. This was a day of decision-making: Should I stay for the conference and help the leaders of our church or obey God's call? Pastor Lee's words echoed in my ears and heart, "Now is the time to move on—do not put it off!" God's commands gave me special strength and courage. I woke up early morning, all set to make the trip to Lee Arrendale, a state prison for women in Georgia.

After picking Carolyn up, we were on our way when, all of a sudden, there was a thick fog; it was so thick that the visibility was zero. I put on the emergency flashers, slowly got over to the right lane, and stopped the car. Then I turned on the defoggers; accidentally, the knuckles of my right fingers hit the wiper switch, and miraculously, the windshield wipers turned on, sweeping across the glass and clearing off all the sediment. Suddenly, the visibility returned, and the fog disappeared. I tell you, it was truly God who saved us from a very serious—if not fatal—accident.

We reached our destination on time, and when I looked at those high wire fences from the outside, it shook me up a bit, but in my mind, I said, "Here I am, Lord!" Once I entered the prison, what a privilege it was! God used me as His vessel to minister to many of the inmates, and I was tremendously blessed when one precious young lady came rushing toward my partner and me, crying, telling us she wanted to accept Jesus Christ as her Savior right now. At the end of the day, another inmate spoke to me and said, "Please, keep coming. Don't stop, for it is very encouraging!"

In preparation for this prison ministry, I had fasted for five days and constantly prayed for months, "Lord, I don't know what to say or how to say it; please, teach me, guide me, and speak through my mouth. Let me see Jesus' face in the inmates," for He said, "I was in prison and you came to Me" (Matthew 25:36c, NKJV). I always prayed an earnest prayer, "Lord, please make use of me, that I would have at least one soul turn to God during this upcoming ministry, for the Scripture says, when one sinner turns to God, in heaven the angels will rejoice with God (Luke 15:10)." As I walked out of the prison, my eyes were filled with tears of joy, for the Lord had truly answered my prayer. I would like to add that the Lord planted the seed in my heart in N. Y., 2001, and nine years later, He made it fruitful in Georgia!

My beloved reader, whenever and wherever you get a chance, I encourage you to serve the Lord with all your mind, with all your heart, and with all your soul, and glorify His name. Do not be afraid of people. You will face many difficult challenges, beginning with your own family. Do not give in. Stand firm and do the will of God; that is our duty. There is nothing in this world more rewarding than to be a servant of the Almighty God—the Creator—the Redeemer.

CHAPTER 7:

THE FULFILLMENT OF THE PROPHECIES REGARDING JESUS' SUFFERING

During Jesus' time, there were no radios or television sets, yet He always seemed to have huge crowds following Him wherever He went. His popularity spread so rapidly that soon, people were following Him not only from village to village and town to town but also from country to country (Mark 3:8; Matthew 4:23–25; Luke 6:17). Sadly, at the same time, animosity began to grow among some of His own people, since they were enraged over His teachings to the point of killing Him (Luke 4:28–30).

Things got so bad, as He was teaching, "the Pharisees and the teachers of the law from every town in Galilee and Judea and from Jerusalem were there" (Luke 5:17, NCV). They were constantly following Jesus, for they had set out on a little fault-finding mission, trying to drum up anything that they could use against Him—it really didn't matter to them whether it was the truth or not. In fact, they had already convinced themselves in their minds that this man was blaspheming (claiming to be equal to God) (Luke 5:21), which at that time was punishable by stoning to death (Leviticus 24:16). Although some of the Jews wanted to kill Him, Jesus continued to teach, preach, heal the sick, and free the demon-possessed. He performed many miraculous signs in public places.

One day, when the Passover feast was approaching (John 6:4), He saw a great multitude coming toward Him. He compassionately asked Phillip, one of the disciples, "Where shall we buy bread, that these may eat?" (John 6:5, NKJV).

Phillip answered, "Two hundred denarii [eight months of salary] worth of bread is not sufficient for them, that every one of them may have a little" (verse 7, NKJV). (Little did he know!)

Andrew, another disciple, spoke up, "There is a lad here who has five barley loaves and two small fish, but what are they among so many?" (verse 9, NKJV). (Little did he know!)

There were about five thousand men in the crowd beside the women and children, according to the Gospel of Matthew 14:21. Jesus told the disciples to have them sit down; He took the loaves and the fish, looked up to heaven, gave thanks, and broke them, and He gave it to the disciples to distribute to the people (Matthew 14:19). The Scripture says everyone ate until they were satisfied—yet there were enough "fragments of the five barley loaves" left over to fill twelve baskets (John 6:13, NKJV). It probably seemed as if this bread would never run out; He could feed the whole world from generation to generation until His second coming. All four Gospels record this miraculous event. (Please read John 6:3–13; Luke 9:10–17; Mark 6:34–44; Matthew 14:13–21.) Oh, what a miracle! Who can perform such marvelous things? Is there any other god? After witnessing this miraculous sign, the people believed that Jesus was the Messiah who was to come, and He knew that they wanted to make Him a King, but He withdrew from them (John 6:14–15).

The day after Jesus did the miraculous sign, the same crowd

THE FULFILLMENT OF THE PROPHECIES

caught up with Him in Capernaum, and they asked Him a casual question (please read John 6:22–25). Then Jesus told them,

> Most assuredly, I say to you, you seek Me, not because you saw the signs, but because you ate of the loaves and were filled. Do not labor for the food which perishes, but for the food which endures to everlasting life, which the Son of Man will give you, because God the Father has set His seal on Him.
>
> **John 6:26–27 (NKJV)**
> **(Emphasis added by the author)**

Jesus is still saying to us, simply, do not work for the food that meets only our physical needs, which perishes, but have the desire for His presence in our daily life by putting the time and effort into studying (eating, as God commanded the prophet Ezekiel [3:3]) His words. This would nurture our souls, and our spirits will live forever!

Jesus continued His missionary work, and His teachings became harder to understand; eventually, most of His disciples deserted Him. The crowd told Him their forefathers received manna from heaven, and they asked Him what sign He would perform so they could believe Him (John 6:30–31). Jesus declared, "I am the bread of life. He who comes to Me shall never hunger, and he who believes in Me shall never thirst" (John 6:35, NKJV). As He continued this same subject, He would interchange the word "bread" with His "flesh" and "blood." and the importance of partaking of His body and blood. He emphasizes the fact that He is from heaven and He is the living bread; those who eat it will have eternal life; if not, they will die. Jesus promised, "He who eats My flesh and drinks My blood abides in Me, and I in him" (verse 56, NKJV). When the people heard this teaching, they were confused, for they could not understand how they could eat His flesh or drink His blood. It is possible that they even thought of it cannibalistic; after hearing these teachings, many of His disciples said, "This teaching is hard. Who can accept it?" (verse 60, NCV). Soon, many of them turned back and no longer followed Him.

In fact, I found myself confused by these teachings until I began studying in preparation for writing this passage. I used to find that when I would come to a portion of Scripture that was hard to understand, I would just skip it. But this time, I continued to study all these verses until the Holy Spirit revealed their true meaning to me. Jesus explained to His disciples, *"It is the Spirit that gives life. The flesh doesn't give life. The words I told you are spirit, and they give life"* (John 6:63 (NCV) (emphasis added by the author). I thanked the Holy Spirit for giving me an understanding of this Scripture. This goes to show you how important it is to study His teachings and write them down on the "tablet of your heart," as Proverbs 7:3 says. That is how He abides in us, and we in Him.

When Jesus realized most of the disciples had left Him except the twelve He had chosen initially, He asked them, "You do not want to leave too, do you?" (verse 67).

Then Simon Peter answered, "Lord, to whom shall we go? You have the words of eternal life. We believe and know that you are the Holy One of God" (John 6:68–69). Do those words uttered by Simon Peter two thousand years ago seem just as real to you today as they were to him back then? I hope so. For me, He is the only One I desire to go to; in fact, I can't even imagine life without Him. The most important thing a person can do in life is to study the Word of God, for Jesus is the *Word*, and His words are Spirit and life-giving; therefore, without Him, there is no eternal life. The more we take in the words, the more we have of God in us.

Jesus came to this world to reveal God's glory (power and authority) so that the people may believe in Him as well as in the One who sent Him, thus glorifying both Father and the Son. Apostle John testifies, "The Word became a human and lived among us.

THE FULFILLMENT OF THE PROPHECIES

We saw his glory—the glory that belongs to the only Son of the Father—and he was full of grace and truth" (John 1:14, NCV). For the first time, God's glory was revealed at the wedding in Cana when He turned the water into wine, and as the apostles witnessed this supernatural, godly power, they believed in Him (please read John 2:1–11).

On another occasion, in the Gospel of John, chapter eleven, he explains there was a man named Lazarus who lived in a village called Bethany, and his two sisters, Martha and Mary, also lived in the same village. One day, Lazarus became critically ill, and the sisters sent the message to Jesus with the hope that the Lord would come right away and heal their brother since He loved the entire family very much (John 11:3, 5, 36). By the time news got to the Lord, He knew Lazarus was already dead (John 11:4, 11–15), and Jesus was nowhere closer to Bethany but "across the Jordan" (John 10:40). Intentionally, He chose to remain at the same place for two more days (11:6), instead of hurrying to get to His loved ones, for Jesus wanted to make sure the Jewish people understood Lazarus had truly died. So, the people around him may believe that Jesus was the Son of God through the miracle He would be performing on the dead man. Thereby, He and the Father would be glorified (John 11:4).

Finally, when Jesus and His disciples arrived, the body had already been placed in the tomb for four days. (For better understanding, please read John 11:1–20.)

At first, Martha met Jesus, and we can see her making faithful statements to the Lord and His encouraging answers in verses 21 through 27 (NCV),

Martha said, "Lord, if you had been here, my brother would not have died. But I know that even now God will give you anything you ask."

Jesus comforted her, "Your brother will rise and live again."

Martha said, "I know that he will rise and live again in the resurrection on the last day."

Jesus affirmed her, "I am the resurrection and the life. Those who believe in me will have life even if they die. And everyone who lives and believes in me will never die. Martha, do you believe this?"

Martha answered, "Yes, Lord. I believe that you are the Christ, the Son of God, the One coming to the world."

There were many Jews gathered at this dead man's house to comfort his family. The sisters guided Jesus to the tomb as He inquired about the location; the crowd that had gathered at the house also followed them.

After they arrived at the burial place, they removed the stone from the entrance of the tomb as He commanded them.

Jesus shouted, "Lazarus, come out!" (verse 43).

Surely, Lazarus came out, still wrapped in the burial linen strips. Most likely, Jesus told His disciples, "Take the cloth off of him and let him go" (verse 44, NCV). After witnessing the miracle Jesus had done, many of the Jews who were there faithfully believed in Him (John 11:45). The others chose to report to the Pharisees the miraculous sign they had just witnessed (verse 46).

The Pharisees and the chief priests, upon hearing the report, immediately called a meeting with the Sanhedrin, the Jewish high court. It was an assembly that consisted of seventy members, including the high priest, the chief priests, the elders of the people, the teachers of the Law, and the families of the high priest.

As the group members gathered, they began asking, "What should we do?" (John 11:47, NCV). They were greatly concerned that the Romans would take away their nation and lose their position if all the people would put their faith in Jesus and follow Him because of His mighty power (verse 48). The high priest at that time, Caiaphas, said, "You people know nothing! You don't realize that it is better for one man to die for the people than for the whole nation to be destroyed" (11:49–50, NCV). Of course, these were not Caiaphas' own words—they were revealed to him by God the Father, according to John 11:51. From that time on, the Sanhedrin conspired to kill Jesus (verse 53). (Please read John 11, the entire chapter, for your understanding.)

THE KING ARRIVES IN ALL OF HIS GLORY

Jesus had been to Jerusalem on several occasions, and yet this visit would be totally different from all the rest; this time, He would be coming in all of His glory. It was close to the time of the Jews' Passover feast, a very special occasion when all the Jews, including those who were scattered throughout the world, gathered in Jerusalem to celebrate.

As Jesus approached Jerusalem, He instructed two of His disciples to bring Him a young donkey that had never been ridden. After they found the colt, they placed their capes on its back in preparation for the King's glorious entrance into the city (Mark 11:2, 7). In the meantime, the crowd heard that Jesus was on His way, so they spread their cloaks/linens and tree branches on the road (Mark 11:8; Matthew 21:8). Also, people carried palm branches to receive Him (John 12:13) just as He came riding by, thus fulfilling the prophecy found in Zechariah 9:9, which is quoted in Matthew 21:5 (NCV), "Tell the people of Jerusalem, 'Your king is coming to you. He is gentle and riding on a donkey, on the colt of a donkey.'" The crowd was so huge since the foreigners who came for the Passover wanted to see the King. They had been told about the miraculous signs He had done and how He raised Lazarus on the fourth day after his death (John 12:17–18). All along the way, the crowds worshiped Him, and they praised Him by shouting in a loud voice,

"Hosanna to the Son of David!"

"Blessed is he who comes in the name of the Lord!"

"Hosanna in the highest!" (Matthew 21:9)

This event is recorded in all four Gospels with slight variations in wording (please read Matthew 21:1–11; Mark 11:1–10; Luke 19:28–38; John 12:12–18).

Sadly, some of the Pharisees were in the crowd, but they were not partakers of this blessed occasion. Instead, they were at a loss and said to themselves, "You can see that nothing is going right for us. Look! The whole world is following him!" (John 12:19, NCV). Then, the Pharisees told Jesus to ask His disciples to stop shouting. But the Lord replied to them, "I tell you, if my followers didn't say these things, then the stones would cry out" (Luke 19:40, NCV). Luke continued and wrote that when Jesus saw Jerusalem, "He wept over it" (verse 41), for the people who were the experts of the Law did not recognize Him as their God, the awaited Messiah, who would bring peace to them. As a result, they would suffer the consequences (for better understanding, please read Luke 19:41–44).

Even today, Christians, rich or poor, famous or unknown, forget the fact that Jesus brought peace and joy to this world. We tend to go after our own feelings and emotions, which leads us to depression, or worse, we take our lives into our own hands. This reminds me of my own situation in 2002 when I consulted with a neurologist for my stiff neck and tightness in my shoulders. This doctor was very friendly, and we had a long conversation. She inquired about my family, and I began to cry when I spoke about my daughter. I was deeply concerned about her being obese and not interested in furthering her education; I was sobbing uncontrollably.

The doctor told me I was depressed, and she gave me a prescription. I was advised to take one pill every day for one month. I filled the prescription, drove to work, and went directly to my

THE FULFILLMENT OF THE PROPHECIES

friend Belinda, a prison minister, good preacher, and prayer warrior. I told her that I needed prayer—that I was depressed. I felt like my emotions were flat, as if my brain was completely empty. I felt like I was on the verge of a collapse. She prayed over me with Bible verses and gave me a few Scriptures to take home. She advised me to pray to Jesus Christ using those verses.

Looking back, I know that this was the day that I completely turned my heart to the Lord, and He took me in His arms. God began working miracles in my life, one after the other. I kept praying using the Scriptures that Belinda gave me, and my Lord and Savior delivered me from the devil. The Word of God is so powerful when you pray faithfully using Scriptures that fit your situation. You will see the miracles working. The Lord said that His Word would not return to Him empty but would accomplish the purpose for which it was sent (Isaiah 55:11). I never took a single pill, but I kept that full bottle as a testimony to myself until March 8, 2006—the day I moved out of the house on Long Island.

My beloved reader, if you know someone suffering from depression, share my story with them, and pray for them as I pray for you. Pray that they will not turn to alcohol or drugs, for these things only temporarily mask the pain and finally lead to destruction. Only God is able to heal the deep, crushing wounds in your heart. So, seek Jesus Christ—He is the healer, the doctor of doctors, the Wonderful Counselor, and He loves you more than your parents love you, more than your siblings, more than your spouse, more than your children, and more than you friends love you, including myself as your friend. I know it is true because I have tasted it. He is available every moment of our lives. Turn your heart toward Him and speak to Him. He is waiting on you.

It touched my heart when I heard of the death of Robin Williams, the actor and comedian. I had never noticed any pride in him; of course, I had seen him only on the big and small screen. As a humble and kind gentleman, he made billions of people laugh, and he demonstrated compassion for children with cancer.

Although this chapter was written in 2011 or 2012, it was only after Mr. Williams' death that the Holy Spirit burdened my heart to write about my past. I pray that God would give His wisdom, knowledge, and understanding to Mr. Williams' children so that they are guided down the right path.

As I was waiting on the Lord to guide me to publish His book, in 2018, two more world-famous celebrities took their precious lives due to depression; first, Kate Spade, followed by Anthony Bourdain. They both abandoned their young daughters, preteens, at an age when they needed their parents the most for protection, guidance, advice, moral support, hugs, love, laughter, and you name it. I wished they had called out to Jesus to come into their hearts; the Lord would have freed them from the demon.

In this world, mostly every day, we all go through difficult times. No one is exempt. Some days are worse than others. Jesus Himself said in Matthew 6:34 not to worry about the next day, for each day has its own trouble. I think that's how God programmed this world so that the people can either use God's wisdom and be an overcomer or use their own will, which is the devil's work for their destruction.

Jesus is inviting every one of us,

> *Come to me, all of you who are tired and have heavy loads, and I will give you rest. Accept my teachings and learn from me, because I am gentle and humble in spirit, and you will find rest for your lives. The burden that I ask you to accept is easy; the load I give you to carry is light.*
>
> **Matthew 11:28–30 (NCV)**
> **(Emphasis added by the author)**

Although Jesus knew He would go through many sufferings, including crucifixion, yet, He wants to give peace to our minds, hearts, and souls, guide us to eternity, and give us everlasting life. What a *loving* God!

THE FULFILLMENT OF THE PROPHECIES

IN HIS MIGHTY POWER, JESUS ENTERS THE TEMPLE

After the great procession in Jerusalem, Jesus went to the temple. In the temple court, He noticed that instead of being clean, holy, and pleasing to God, it had become quite filthy. Most likely, the chief priests and the teachers of the Law had allowed it to turn into a commercial place. The merchants were selling young bulls, sheep, and doves in the temple courts (John 2:14) so that those who couldn't bring their offerings with them could purchase and use them for the annual sacrifices, especially during the week of Passover. The money changers had set up their booths to make it even more convenient for the foreigners to exchange their money for local currency to pay their temple tax, as well as to buy the sacrificial animals.

Jesus became furious at the sight of His Father's house being degraded—in fact, in His righteous indignation, "Jesus made a whip out of cords" (John 2:15, NCV) and drove the animals out of the area. In His fervor, He overturned the tables of the money changers and scattered their funds all over, and He asked those who sold the doves to take them away (please read John 2:13–16). Although He did all this right in front of His enemies, they dared not lay a hand on Him. Jesus said to them, "It is written, 'My house is a house of prayer,' but you have made it a 'den of thieves'" (Luke 19:46, NKJV). Jesus said, "It is written." My friend, I ask you a question, "Do you know where it is written?" (if you don't, please read Isaiah 56:7).

I was editing the above portion on January 2, 2016; only then the Holy Spirit gave me a clear understanding of what it meant when the twelve-year-old boy Jesus asked His earthly parents, "Why did you seek Me? Did you not know that I must be about My Father's business?" (Luke 2:49, NKJV). Which showed, at very young age, Jesus began His missionary work here at His Father's house and completed it at this very temple (Luke 21:37–38).

Even today, if we go to another country, we cannot use our own money. We must exchange what we have for whatever is acceptable in that particular locale. Although the need to exchange currency remains the same today as it did back then, you'll never find it done in a church or temple, nor in any worshiping place. I know some Hindus who believe that cows are sacred animals, and they worship them, yet I don't believe that they would allow the cows to enter their temples.

THE JERUSALEM TEMPLES

Today, places of worship, such as temples, synagogues, churches, and mosques, are designed and built by engineers and architects using plans and blueprints; construction can only begin after the city completes its inspections, which are done to make sure the projects will meet their standards and codes. But the temple of Jerusalem was unique because God Almighty was its architect, engineer, designer, and planner.

The first Jerusalem temple was built in BC 959 by King Solomon, four hundred and eighty-seven years after the Israelites had returned from Egypt (1 Kings 6:1, 37–38). Although his father, David, had the desire to build it, God opposed this and said it would be his son who would build the temple for Him; "Who will come from your own body …He is the one who will build a house for my name" (2 Samuel 7:12d, 13a). It only took seven years for Solomon to build the temple (1 Kings 6:38) because his father had prepared and kept most of all the materials and articles needed for constructing the temple. David had even made a table of organization showing the positions and the functions of each person involved in building God's temple, as well as serving there (please

THE FULFILLMENT OF THE PROPHECIES

read 1 Chronicles 22:1–4, 14–19; and chapters 23–29:9). He was very concerned about his son being too young and inexperienced to take up this profound responsibility, and he wanted God's temple to be very magnificent and famous in the world, so he did all of the above to help his son (1 Chronicles 22:5). David testified that God gave him the full plans and understanding to build this temple, "*'All this,' said David, 'the LORD made me understand in writing, by His hand upon me, all the works of these plans'*" (1 Chronicles 28:19, NKJV) (emphasis added by the author). Then David gave his son Solomon all the plans that God had put in his heart. (Please read 1 Chronicles 28:9–18 and pay attention to verses 11 and 12.)

Once the building was complete, the priests brought in the ark of the covenant (1 Kings 8:6). The ark was made by Moses; it was also according to God's plans and instructions. (Please read Exodus 25:9–16.) It contained the two stone tablets upon which the Lord Himself had written the ten commandments (Exodus 25:21, 31:18; 1 Kings 8:9), and they placed the ark in the inner sanctuary of the temple, the Most Holy Place. Soon, the glory of the Lord came in and filled up the temple in the form of a cloud (1 Kings 8:10–11). After Solomon completed the prayers and sacrifices for the dedication, God appeared to him and said,

> *I have heard your prayer and your supplication that you have made before Me; I have consecrated this house which you have built to put My name there forever, and My eyes and My heart will be there perpetually.*
>
> **1 Kings 9:3 (NKJV)**
> **(Emphasis added by the author)**

That showed what a holy place that was!

Although David, a man after God's own heart, had the desire to build a temple for the Lord, God opposed it. Don't you want to know why? I'm sure your heart is very eager to know, so please open your Bible to 1 Kings chapter five and read verses three to five; you will find the answer. And my heart desires for you to read 1 Kings chapters 5–6, 7:13 through the end of the chapter and grasp the depth of the works done by this young king, Solomon! His mind, heart, soul, and wisdom were completely devoted to doing a very precise, detailed, expensive, and beautiful work on the Lord's temple. Can you imagine the manpower he needed to construct this house of prayer? Just think, hiring 80,000 men to cut out the stones alone! This temple had three parts: The outer court, where the Gentiles worshiped; the inner sanctuary, or the Holy place; and the innermost place, or Holy of the Holiest, where the ark of the covenant was placed. And it also had three stories in some areas of the building: first, second, and third floors. What a magnificent structure!

Nearly four centuries later, in BC 586, the above-mentioned temple was destroyed by Nebuchadnezzar, a Gentile, the king of Babylon, today's Iraq. Please read the book of Jeremiah to learn why God brought this disaster to the Israelites. Seventy years later, God prepared the hearts of three Gentile kings, Cyrus, Darius, and Artaxerxes, to help the Israelites rebuild the temple. Can you imagine, over a century and a half prior to it, God already had foretold that Cyrus would be the one to initiate rebuilding the temple, as well as Jerusalem (Isaiah 44:28). This is to show the world that God is in control of everyone, whether Jew or Gentile. Thus, the second temple was built in BC 516, as decreed by King Cyrus, under the guidance of prophets Haggai and Zechariah, as commanded by God (Ezra 5:1–2, 6:14–15). For better understanding, please read Ezra chapters 1–6; Haggai 1–2:9; Zechariah 1:16, 6:15. We can see King Cyrus' own words,

> *Thus says Cyrus king of Persia: All the kingdoms of the earth the LORD God of heaven has given me. And He has commanded me to build Him a house at*

Jerusalem which is in Judah. Who is among you of all His people? May the LORD his God be with him, and let him go up!

2 Chronicles 36:23 (NKJV)
(Emphasis added by the author)

The Lord promised to Haggai, we read in this prophet's book 2:7c–9, that this house will be filled with His glory and will be greater glory than the previous one!

According to the book of Hebrews, this time, the ark of the covenant contained the following, "The gold jar of manna, Aaron's staff that had budded, and the stone tablets of the covenant" (Hebrews 9:4). It took forty-six years to complete this temple as per the Jews of Jesus' time (John 2:20). This was the very temple where boy Jesus spent three days with the teachers of the Law while His earthly parents, Mary and Joseph, were searching for Him (Luke 2:45–46). As I was reviewing this portion today, 11/25/2023, a thought came to my heart as to why God the Father foretold, "The glory of this present house will be greater than the glory of the former house" (Haggai 2:9). Is it because God's presents would be here not as a cloud, but in human flesh, the Son of God, the Prince of Peace would be in this temple doing the Father's will!

I hope that perhaps by reading the above information, you will have more insight as to why Jesus was so upset when He entered the temple and saw how the people had desecrated God's dwelling place.

The History of the Passover

While still childless, and before he became known as Abraham, God foretold Abram that for four hundred years, his descendants would be enslaved in a foreign land (Genesis 15:13); but afterward, He would restore what He had promised to Abram

(Genesis 15:16–21; 12:6–7; 13:12a, 14–15): a land flowing with milk and honey (Exodus 3:8). What an awesome God! Who can fathom what His thoughts or plans are for each one of us and even for those who are not yet born? He is so faithful; He always fulfills His promises.

Just as God foretold, the Israelites were slaves in Egypt for four centuries. The Lord became very concerned when He saw their misery and suffering and heard their cry, so He decided to deliver them from their bondage. Thus, He chose Moses, along with his brother, Aaron, to accomplish the mission (please read Exodus chapters 3–4:17 to learn about the conversation between God and Moses). God was always with them, and He did at least ten miraculous signs and wonders in Egypt for the destruction of the slave drivers and the country as a whole.

The last one was the killing of all the firstborn sons (Exodus 11:1, 4–6), beginning with the son of Pharaoh, the ruler of Egypt, to the maidservants and even extending to the firstborn male cattle. In order to save the Israelites (please read Exodus chapter 12), the whole community was instructed to do the following as they had been commanded by God: At twilight, they were to slaughter a one-year-old male sheep or goat without defect or blemish. In order to distinguish their homes from the Egyptians' homes, the Israelites were to apply some blood from the same animal to the top and sides of the doorframe. Then, on that same night, they were to roast and eat the meat with bitter herbs (reminding them of their bitter experiences in Egypt), along with bread made without yeast (unleavened bread, for there wasn't enough time to ferment the dough). They were also told, "Eat it in haste [hurry]; it is the LORD's Passover" (Exodus 12:11d). At midnight, God would send out "a band of destroying angels" (Psalm 78:49c) to pass through Egypt and strike down every firstborn, but the angels would pass over (protect) the houses that had blood on the door frame. Thus, all of the Egyptian firstborns were killed, including Pharaoh's, but

THE FULFILLMENT OF THE PROPHECIES

just as God had promised, the Israelites' were spared.

Due to the catastrophic devastation, the whole country was mourning and wailing. Because he feared God's wrath, hardhearted Pharaoh granted permission for Moses and all the Israelites to leave Egypt the very same night (Exodus 12:31). Although the number of women and children was not accounted for in the biblical record, there were about six hundred thousand men (Exodus 12:37, 38:26). That very night, after four hundred thirty years in Egypt (Exodus 12:40–41), God delivered the Israelites out of Egypt. In order for His people to travel through the Red Sea, He parted the waters and turned the sea into dry land with His mighty power (Exodus 14:21–22).

Not only did He make the walls of water in the Red Sea (Exodus 14:22), but the angel of protection and God Himself were there in the form of a pillar of fire and cloud in front of the Israelites to lead and guide them in their journey. But when the angel saw the Egyptian army following the Israelites, both the angel and the pillar of cloud moved behind them, between the Israeli and the Egyptian armies, and protected His people (14:19–20). What an amazing and loving God of Abraham, Isaac, and Jacob! At this, the Holy Spirit reminded me of what Jesus spoke of their descendants in Matthew 23:37 and Luke 13:34; it was exactly like a hen would gather her chicks and protect them under her wings. (Exodus 14 is a must-read chapter to understand the miraculous wonders God did in order to protect and bring all His people from Egypt; pay close attention to verses 15–31.)

The Passover is the most significant event in the Old Testament, for God commanded the people to celebrate it as a festival to Him, from generation to generation, during the first month (according to the Jewish calendar) every year for seven days as a reminder of God's faithfulness in redeeming them from their bondage in Egypt. They were to kill Passover lamb every year, to have no yeast in the house on those seven days, or to eat anything that contained yeast (Exodus 13:3–10). (Please read Exodus chapters 3–14 to learn the entire plans and wondrous works of God in fulfilling His promise to Abram.)

Even Jesus, being God Himself, did not fail to obey that command; in fact, we notice in the Gospel of Luke that at the age of twelve, He arrived with His parents at the Jerusalem temple to celebrate Passover, and as an adult, He kept that same reverence for His Father and attended this feast every year (John 2:13–16; 6:4; 11:55–12:1; 13:1). Using these passages in John, biblical scholars calculated that the Lord's ministry had to be approximately three to three and a half years.

Now, I am going to ask all of my readers to take a moment before you go on reading the rest of the chapter and ask Father God to open up your heart in order to help you grasp the real meaning of what these next few sentences have to say. Jesus knew, while He was still up in heaven, what He would be going through in His humanity during His time on Earth. Due to the fact that He was God, He was completely aware of all that He would have to suffer: being flogged, spit on, insulted, mocked, beaten, abused, and ultimately hung by His precious hands and feet to a cruel cross. Those same hands that healed the sick, encouraged the fainthearted, and soothed those troubled souls, and those same feet that carried Him miles and miles to preach the good news of the kingdom of God to the poor and to the captives. Despite knowing all of the torment and suffering that He would have to endure, Jesus still chose to set aside His kingship in order to come down to Earth and save sinners like you and me, not because we deserved it, but simply because of His great love and compassion for us. We must remember that during His time on Earth, because of His humanity, He had the same feelings and emotions that we have, and He felt pain the same way that we feel it.

THE FULFILLMENT OF THE PROPHECIES

Since all the prophecies that had been prophesied by the prophets and psalmists still had to be fulfilled, Jesus and His disciples had to set out for Jerusalem during His last days (please read Mark 10:32–34; Luke 18:31–33), where He would continue His missionary work.

Jesus knew that His time on Earth was drawing to a close (John 13:1), and His main desire was to have the Passover supper with the disciples. He told Peter and John to go into the city and make the preparations for this final feast, known as the Last Supper or the Lord's Supper. He informed them that they were going to find a man with a water pitcher (although in those days, it was traditionally the women's job to carry water from the well—even today, in my native village, it is the ladies' work); he would take them to a house with a large upper room that was completely furnished. There they were to begin preparing for the meal (Mark 14:12–16; Matthew 26:17–19; Luke 22:7–13). Had God not been the disciples' guide, all this could have been a very difficult assignment due to the size of the city and the massive crowds, for the Jews from all over the world were gathered there for the Passover.

In the evening, Jesus and all His disciples were reclining and fellowshipping at the table, and He lovingly said that He had longed to eat this Passover together with them before the time of His suffering (Luke 22:14–15). Jesus also promised them that He would never eat it again until they could partake of it together in the kingdom of God; likewise, the wine also (Luke 22:16–18; also recorded in Mark 14:25; Matthew 26:29 with a slight difference).

John 13:1–17 notes that because of His great love, Jesus humbly chose to take on the role of a servant and wash the disciples' feet before the evening meal. He knew very soon He would be going back to His heavenly home, and before He left, He wanted His followers to understand all that leadership entailed. First and foremost comes the responsibility to manifest the love of God by modeling servant behavior, and it needs to be carried out with no hint of power or pride. He also stressed that the gospel itself is a way of life to be lived, not simply an ideal to be thought about. A thought, until it is put into action, is worthless, and the motivation for our actions should be love—a love for God and for our fellow man.

Jesus returned to His seat after washing their feet (John 13:12). His friends were all enjoying the meal when He said, "I tell you the truth, one of you will betray me" (Matthew 26:21).

Upon hearing this, they were saddened and shocked. One by one, they said to Him, "Surely not I, Lord?" (Matthew 26:22).

Jesus replied, "It is one of the Twelve, one who dips bread into the bowl with me" (Mark 14:20). Here, one of the prophecies of David was fulfilled, "Even my close friend, whom I trusted, he who shared my bread, has lifted up his heel against me" (Psalm 41:9). (This is quoted in John 13:18.)

As their conversation continued, Jesus said, "The Son of Man will go just as it is written about him. But woe to that man who betrays the Son of Man! It would be better for him if he had not been born" (Matthew 26:24 and Mark 14:21). (Luke recorded this with slight variation in his book 22:21–22.) Jesus was affirming to His disciples and to us that this man's woeful decision would cause him horrible punishment; eternally, he is dead, like a dead man walking; it would have been better if he had never been born. But Jesus will go back to His Father as it had been prophesied. Jesus was revealing to them about His resurrection and ascension.

Right away, Judas—the disciple who had already made a deal with the chief priests for thirty pieces of silver (Matthew 26:14–16; Mark 14:10–11; Luke 22:2–6; John 13:2) that he would betray his Master—asked, "Surely not I, Rabbi?" (Matthew 26:25). Immediately Jesus replied in the same verse, "Yes, it is you."

While they were eating, "[Jesus] took bread, gave thanks and broke it, and gave it to them, saying, 'This is my body given for you; do this in remembrance of me'" (Luke 22:19). And after they had finished the meal, He took the cup of wine, gave thanks, and offered it to them saying, "This cup is *the new covenant in my blood*, which is poured out for you" (Luke 22:20) (emphasis added by the author). (Recorded in Matthew 26:26–28; Mark 14:22–24.) Although all four Gospels record the importance of partaking in His body and blood, Apostle John's version (6:50–58) is very different from the first three synoptic Gospels. Jesus commanded the disciples, "Do this in remembrance of me" (Luke 22:19). This is why, even today, Christians are obedient to His command. They consecrate the bread and wine and celebrate Holy Communion (Eucharist) on the Lord's Day (Sundays) and on special occasions.

The breaking of the bread represented the upcoming violent death of our Savior, as His body would be broken for our iniquities. Likewise, the wine was symbolic of Jesus' blood, which would be shed on the cross for the forgiveness of man's sin.

JESUS' BODY AND BLOOD

This chapter was written either in the year 2011 or 2012. As I waited for the timing of His book to be published, I was prompted in my spirit with a desire to read and study the New Testament one chapter a day. In the spring of 2021, I began to study the Gospel of Apostle John, for to me, it was the most difficult book to understand. I continued to study the books up to the first Epistles of Corinthians. As I read chapter 11 of 1 Corinthians, I noticed the emphasis that was put on Christians and how they must prepare their hearts and conducts when receiving Jesus' body and blood. Also, I noticed the consequences they could receive if acknowledgment was not made that this was the body and blood of Jesus. Please read 1 Corinthians 11:20 through the end and pay close attention to verses 23–31. Although this letter was written in the first century for a certain people, it is for all Christians all over the world and all the generations up to the return of our Lord.

Upon studying this passage, a thought came to my heart to read the Last Supper, which I wrote a few years ago. I began to read chapter 7, "The Fulfillment of the Prophecies Regarding Jesus' Suffering and Death," in August of 2021. My eyes caught the exact subject God had impressed in my heart, and I thought to myself how profound this teaching was and how poorly I wrote it down. At this, I was embarrassed but not ashamed, for as I mentioned before, I'm poor in language and immature in Scripture. Someone with a biblical scholar would have been better qualified than me.

If you read chapter 5, "What Was the Purpose of His Coming?" you will notice Jesus taught many subjects, including the Beatitudes, recorded in Matthew chapters 5 through 7. None of those subjects He gave great emphasis as He did on His body and blood. On August 28, 2021, I felt empowered by the Spirit of God. It was the day He opened my inner eyes to a deeper understanding of this subject. Jesus gave much emphasis on the importance and benefits of eating His body and drinking His blood.

Let us go to the book of Apostle John, chapter 6, and study verses 27–58. As I studied these verses, I noticed countless times how Jesus repeatedly said, "I AM," "My," and words like, "Flesh, bread, body, blood, eat, drink, believe, not die, may live, will have eternal life, everlasting life, will raise him up on the last day." He also said, "I am the bread that came down from heaven, 'the living bread,' 'the true bread.' 'The bread of life.'" Jesus again emphasized in verses 53 and 56, *"Unless you eat the flesh of the Son of Man and drink his blood, you have no life in you. ...Whoever eats my flesh and drinks my blood remains in me, and I in him"* (emphasis added by the author).

Today I realized how unlearned I was in this subject matter

THE FULFILLMENT OF THE PROPHECIES

of John's writing. I was as blind as the Jews in the days of Jesus who questioned themselves, "How can this man give us his flesh to eat?" (John 6:52). Let us study the synoptical Gospels, Matthew 26:26–28; Mark 14:22–24; Luke 22:19–20 to better understand the clear picture of the above question.

Please notice that while Jesus and the apostles were eating the Passover meal, the Lord took the bread, gave thanks, broke it, and gave it to the disciples. He then said, "This is my body given for you; do this in remembrance of me" (Luke 22:19). After the supper, He took the cup and said, "This cup is the new covenant in my blood, which is poured out for you" (verse 20). The Gospel of Matthew records this with a slight difference. Jesus said, "Drink from it, all of you. This is my blood of the covenant, which is poured out for many for the forgiveness of sins" (Matthew 26:27–28).

As we see, Jesus did not cut open His body to give His flesh or His blood to His disciples. It was unleavened bread and wine, which symbolized His body and blood. He blessed them both in a distinctive way. Jesus commanded them to do this in remembrance of Him, and in turn, the apostles passed it on to us. That means, whenever we receive His body and blood, meditate in our hearts, "Jesus died on the cross for our sins" (see 1 Corinthians 11:26). Had not the Holy Spirit impressed in my heart the reference apostle Paul had made in 1 Corinthians 11:23, *"For I received from the Lord what I also passed on to you"* (emphasis added by the author), I would not have had the audacity to write on this subject. This was proclaimed not only for the first-century Christians but also the twenty-first-century Christians and beyond until the return of Jesus.

I assure you firsthand learning will certainly increase your faith! I recommend you to study 1 Corinthians 11:23–31, John 6:32–58, and the Last Supper in the synoptical Gospels, before you participate or receive Jesus' body and blood/the Holy Communion.

THE TRIAL

That same Thursday evening, after having the Passover supper, they sang a hymn and departed for the Mount of Olives. While they were on their way, Jesus told Peter, "This very night, before the rooster crows, you will disown me three times" (Matthew 26:34). Peter was shocked to hear Jesus say such a thing, immediately he told the Lord, in the next verse, even if it cost his life, he would never deny Him.

When they arrived at the Garden of Gethsemane, He told the disciples to wait there while He went to pray; when He left, He took Peter, James, and John, instructing them to stay awake with Him. Jesus went on alone a little farther, fell face down on the ground, and prayed, "O My Father, if it is possible, let this cup pass from Me; nevertheless, not as I will, but as You will" (Matthew 26:39, NKJV). Jesus was exceedingly troubled, for He knew that shortly, He would be going through an indescribable painful death, and still, He was determined to do His Father's will: to reconcile the fallen humanity with Father. (Please read Romans 5:10–11 for a better understanding.)

Suddenly, an angel appeared and strengthened Him. He continued praying more earnestly, "His sweat was like drops of blood falling to the ground" (Luke 22:44b). When Jesus got up from prayer and went back to those three disciples and found them asleep, He asked, "Could you men not keep watch with me for one hour?" "Watch and pray, so that you will not fall into temptation. The spirit is willing, but the body is weak" (Matthew 26:40–41). Three times He repeatedly went to His Father and prayed almost the same prayer, and each time He returned, the disciples were sound asleep. The third time when He returned, Jesus woke them up and told them the time had come for Him to give Himself into the hands of the sinners. (Please read Matthew 26:42–46; Mark

THE FULFILLMENT OF THE PROPHECIES

14:32–42.)

While Jesus was speaking, Judas came with "a crowd armed with swords and clubs" (Mark 14:43) sent by the Sanhedrin. Judas had prearranged a plan—that he would kiss the one whom they were to arrest. So, he went to his Master and betrayed the Son of Man with a kiss; thus, Jesus was immediately arrested. (Please read Matthew 26:47–56.) During this time of chaos, all the disciples rapidly dispersed and deserted Him, except John and Peter. However, that same night, Peter denied Jesus three times, just as predicted (please read Matthew 26:69–75; John 18:16–18, 25–27). John, who had the privilege of knowing the high priest, faced no problem. He remained faithfully close to his Savior the entire time and witnessed all the sufferings Jesus had endured (John 18:15–16, 19:35).

The men who arrested Jesus brought Him to the Jewish high court, the Sanhedrin (Mark 14:53). They were seeking evidence against Jesus so they could put Him to death, but they found nothing. Although some chose to make false accusations against Him, He remained silent, but soon, false witnesses came forward and said they heard Him say, "I am able to destroy the temple of God and rebuild it in three days" (Matthew 26:61). They misunderstood the Lord's figurative speech. Jesus was actually speaking of His death and resurrection, but they assumed that He was talking about rebuilding the Jerusalem temple. The people couldn't help wondering how this man could rebuild in three days what had taken man forty-six years to build (John 2:20).

Although I had heard from various biblical scholars that Jesus was speaking of His death, burial, and resurrection—He would be killed and would rise on the third day—as I was writing this portion, I became acutely aware that I didn't understand this matter enough to explain it to anyone. As I spoke to the Lord about it, He took my mind to what the apostle Paul had said, "Do you not know that your body is a temple of the Holy Spirit, who is in you, whom you have received from God?" (1 Corinthians 6:19). I then understood God the Father and the Holy Spirit indwelt Jesus at all times, so His body was the temple. Thank You, God Almighty, for this revelation.

The entire Sanhedrin continued their efforts, trying to stir up trouble in order to make His death certain because of their jealousy and fear that He might eventually become their ruler due to the size of the crowds that were following Him, and His popularity continued to grow. The fury of the high priest reached volcanic proportions when Jesus stood before them and said, "But I say to all of you: In the future you will see the Son of Man sitting at the right hand of the Mighty One and coming on the clouds of heaven" (Matthew 26:64b).

"Then the high priest tore his clothes and said, 'He has spoken blasphemy! Why do we need any more witnesses? Look, now you have heard the blasphemy. What do you think?'" (Matthew 26:65–66).

In the same verse, everyone replied, "He is worthy of death."

Despite the verdict, Roman law prohibited them from putting a person to death (John 18:31b), so they waited for daybreak. Those who had been put in charge of guarding the Lord chose to blindfold, mock, beat, insult Him, spit on Him, and strike Him with their fists (Luke 22:63–64; Mark 14:65).

Everything began to fall into place in Jerusalem, just as Jesus predicted, "The Son of Man will be betrayed to the chief priests and the teachers of the law. They will condemn him to death and will turn him over to the Gentiles to be mocked and flogged and crucified" (Matthew 20:18–19a). (Also recorded in Mark 10:33–34a; Luke 18:31–32.)

Early Friday morning, the assembly handed Jesus over to Pi-

THE FULFILLMENT OF THE PROPHECIES

late (a Gentile), who was the governor of Judea, that he might sentence Him to death. When Pilate began his interrogation, he immediately asked Jesus, "Are you the king of the Jews?" "Yes, it is as you say," Jesus responded (Luke 23:3; Matthew 27:11). The chief priests made many accusations against Jesus, but He did not utter a word, which amazed Pilate. He understood they were jealous of Him (Matthew 27:12–14, 18). The governor didn't find any basis for a charge against Him. He found out that Jesus was from Galilee, the jurisdiction of Herod, who happened to be in Jerusalem on that day. Jesus was taken to Herod for trial, but once again, no verdict worthy of the death penalty could be found (please read Luke 23:5–11).

Pilate found himself in a very difficult situation when Jesus was returned to him, for he knew through his wife that He was not only innocent of any crime, but He was a holy man as well (Matthew 27:19). Meanwhile, the crowd continued to shout, "Crucify him, crucify him!" (verses 22–23; Luke 23:21).

We read in the Holy Bible that when the high priest and the chief priests continued their accusations against Jesus, He remained silent (Matthew 26:62–63a; Mark 15:3–5). He didn't utter a word to Herod the governor's questions (Luke 23:8–11). Jesus was not answering some of Pilate's questions either (John 19:9), so the governor asked Him, "Do you refuse to speak to me? ...Don't you realize I have power either to free you or to crucify you?" (John 19:10).

Jesus told him, "You would have no power over me if it were not given to you from above [from God]" (John 19:11a).

Are we not like Pilate? When we harbor pride in our hearts, do we not say, or at least think, "Do you not know who I am and what I am capable of doing?" Do we ever realize that it is only by the grace of God that we have whatever position we may have obtained in life? For the Lord gives us all that we have and makes us into whatever we are to glorify Himself in and through us.

During those days, it was the governor's custom to release a prisoner every year at the time of the Passover feast. Pilate gave the Jewish authorities and the people the opportunity to make that choice. But instead of Jesus, they selected Barabbas, a notorious criminal (Matthew 27:15–16, 20). Although Pilate let them have it their way, he told the Jews that he would have no part in this innocent man's blood. He then took water and washed his hands. This symbolic act seemed to stir up their fury all the more. In their wrath, they were driven to the point of bringing a curse down upon themselves and their children by shouting, "Let his blood be on us and on our children!" (Matthew 27:25). (For better understanding, please read Matthew 27:15–25; Luke 23:13–25.)

Finally, Pilate chose to release Barabbas, had Jesus flogged, and ordered Him to be crucified. There is no indication of how many times Jesus was flogged, but the Jewish law permitted the criminal could be flogged as the crime deserves, but no more than forty times (Deuteronomy 25:1–3). Apostle Paul clearly stated in 2 Corinthians 11:24 that he was flogged thirty-nine times for the gospel. Probably, that is the reason why the Christians believe Jesus was flogged thirty-nine times. The soldiers (the Gentiles) would strip Jesus, secure the hands in metal hoops, and they would flog with a whip that was made of several pieces of leather studded with sharp metal hooks at the ends. With each lash, the skin opened, and muscle tore apart; He bled severely and suffered excruciating pain.

CHAPTER 8:

THE CRUCIFIXION

After they'd flogged Him, the Roman soldiers brought Jesus into a place called "Praetorium" Matthew 27:27; Mark 15:16; Governor's "palace," John 19:9a, or the headquarters of the army where many soldiers were gathered. They stripped the King and then put a purple robe on Him, representing royalty, but they were truly insulting Him. Then they placed a crown made of thorns on Jesus' head (John 19:2) and began to call out, "Hail, king of the Jews!" (John 19:3). And they repeatedly abused Him physically and mentally (for better understanding, please read Matthew 27:27–31; Mark 15:16–20). I don't know what kind of thorn bushes they used. God gave me this thought today (March 14, 2016): Have you ever walked in a rose garden, and a thorn from one of the branches accidentally caught your finger and caused you aching pain, and you began to bleed? Imagine then how painful and how much loss of blood it must have been when the soldiers twisted together a few thorny branches without the leaves and pushed them down around His head to be secured. (Thank You, my Father, for today's teaching.)

The soldiers took off the robe and put on His clothes; then they led Him to a place called "Golgotha," an Aramaic word or "Calvary" in Latin, which means "the place of the skull" (John 19:17). It was customary in those days for criminals to carry their own cross for their crucifixion, so did our Savior (John 19:17). Remember, Jesus was already bleeding and in severe pain from the thorns on His head and from the wounds that had been inflicted all over His body from flogging; thus, His physical strength was almost gone, and He began frequently falling along the way. At last, the soldiers noticed that the King could no longer carry His cross, so they made Simon from Cyrene carry it (Mark 15:21; Matthew 27:32; Luke 23:26).

There were crowds of people; among them were women, including those who faithfully followed Jesus from Galilee. They were brokenhearted and mourned and wailed at His unjust suffering. When Jesus looked at them and saw them crying, He said to them, "Daughters of Jerusalem, do not weep for me; weep for yourselves and for your children" (Luke 23:28). Jesus continued, "For men do these things when the tree is green, what will happen when it is dry?" (verse 31). He was warning them not to feel pity for Him, for He would be victorious at His resurrection, but they and their generations would go through many trials and tribulations in His absence. In other words, keep the faith and be prepared.

Today, Jesus tells us also cry for ourselves, our children, and the generation to come, until His return, for dreadful days are ahead of us. Stand firm in Him so no one will fall away.

Once Jesus arrived at Golgotha, He was secured to the wooden cross by piercing both His palms and His feet with huge nails that were hammered into the cross. Then, they dug a hole in the ground, where the soldiers would place the base of the cross so it would stand firm. In response to Pilate's orders, a plaque reading, "JESUS OF NAZARETH, THE KING OF THE JEWS" was attached at the top of His cross (John 19:19). It was written in all three languages: Aramaic for the Jews, Latin for the Romans, and Greek, which was the common language used in the Roman Empire.

Jesus, our Savior, was crucified along with two thieves, one on His left side and the other on His right (Matthew 27:38). As He hung on the cross, from the third hour (9 a.m.) until the ninth hour (3 p.m.), the entire six-hour period, it was nonstop humiliation. He was mocked, insulted, and challenged by His enemies, saying, "If You are the Son of God, come down from the cross. ...He saved others; Himself He cannot save. If He is the King of Israel, let Him now come down from the cross, and we will believe Him" (Matthew 27:40, 42, NKJV). The crowd never stopped their abuse. Even one of the thieves hanging beside Him yelled, "If You are the Christ, save Yourself and us" (Luke 23:39, NKJV).

I might add what I had learned from a Theologian,

When Adam sinned, he realized he was naked, for no longer he had God's glorious covering, so felt shame and hid behind the tree. Therefore, Jesus had to hang naked in front of the tree, suffering shame to take away the sins of the world, so we will get back that glorious covering again.

Apostle Paul stated, "Will transform our lowly bodies so that they will be like his glorious body" (Philippians 3:21b). Please read verses 20–21 for better understanding.

The one who had never sinned (unblemished) carried the world's sin on the cross. He hung there only on three nails; He blood and died in our place. Thus, Jesus executed the new covenant and fulfilled His ultimate purpose for coming to Earth. "For Christ died for sins once for all, the righteous for the unrighteous, to bring you to God" (1 Peter 3:18). "Once for all" meant Jesus died for all generations, starting with Adam, the past, present, and the future generation. Apostle Paul wrote, "For as by one man's [Adam's] disobedience many were made sinners, so also by one

JESUS, THE KING OF KINGS

Man's [Jesus'] obedience many will be made righteous" (Romans 5:19, NKJV). Death by crucifixion was considered to be the longest hours of suffocation and the most excruciatingly painful death ever carried out by men; it was also a curse (Deuteronomy 21:23; Galatians 3:13).

As Jesus shed His blood and died on the cross, He fulfilled what the Lord had foretold, "The hour has come for the Son of Man to be glorified. I tell you the truth, unless a kernel of wheat falls to the ground and dies, it remains only a single seed. But if it dies, it produces many seeds" (John 12:23–24). Thus, Jesus became the final sacrificial Lamb, and abolished all the animal sacrifices (Hebrews 8:13; 9:12, 26). Also fulfilled what was proclaimed by John the Baptist, "Behold! The Lamb of God who takes away the sin of the world!" (John 1:29, NKJV).

Images of a nail used for crucifixion, and a thorny crown that was placed on Jesus' head.

I hope you're getting a very clear picture of what Jesus, the King of kings, went through in order to save sinners like you and me; if this explanation is not sufficient to feel deep in your heart, I suggest that you watch *The Passion of the Christ*, a film directed by Mel Gibson.

THE CRUCIFIXION

Image of Jesus hanging on a wooden Cross by three nails.

As I was working on the above passage and putting my thoughts together, I couldn't help thinking about Mr. Gibson. How wonderful it would have been if he had produced a second movie on the disciples, on how faithfully they continued to live their lives even after Jesus' death and resurrection. They preached the good news (the Gospel) to a lost and dying world. They did many wonders and miracles by the power of the Holy Spirit, and yet, they were beaten, tortured, imprisoned, and ultimately martyred for their faith. Stop and think about it: How awesome would it have been for the world to have had an opportunity to know that it was only due to the great faith and love these men had for God that we have the gospel available to us today? Otherwise, how would we have had that blessing? I hope and pray that one day, either he or someone else in Hollywood will produce a movie about "The thirteen Jewish men" who gave up their lives in order to be obedient to Jesus' commission (please read Acts 1:8; Matthew 28:18–20; Mark 16:15–18; Luke 24:46–49).

You may wonder how there were thirteen disciples. Of course, Judas Iscariot betrayed Jesus and hung himself (Matthew 27:3–5). After Jesus' death, resurrection, and ascension, Matthias was chosen in Judas' place (please read Acts 1:15–26). Later on, the Lord Himself chose Saul, the destroyer of Christians, to be His disciple (please read Acts 9:1–16; Galatians 1:11–24), whose name was changed to Paul. He became the pillar of the early church, an apostle to the Gentiles, preached the gospel in many countries, and wrote one-third of the New Testament.

All took place just as the Father had planned, for He revealed it to the prophets, who foretold it in the Old Testament. Some of the prophecies and their fulfillment are listed below:

THE CRUCIFIXION

Prophecy	Fulfillment
"Dogs have surrounded me; a band of evil men has encircled me" (Psalm 22:16a and b).	Matthew 27:27
"They have pierced my hands and my feet" (Psalm 22:16c).	Mark 15:25; Luke 23:33a; John 19:18a
"But He was pierced for our transgressions" (Isaiah 53:5a).	John 19:34
"They divided my garments among them and cast lots for my clothing" (Psalm 22:18).	John 19:23–24; Matthew 27:35
"They put gall in my food and gave me vinegar for my thirst" (Psalm 69:21).	Matthew 27:34; John 19:28–29
"The kings of the earth take their stand and the rulers gather together against the LORD and against his Anointed One" (Psalm 2:2).	Matthew 26:57, 59–68; 27:1–2, 11–14; Luke 22:66–71, 23:1–12
"I am an object of scorn to my accusers; when they see me, they shake their heads" (Psalm 109:25).	Matthew 27:39
"All who see me mock me; they hurl insults, shaking their heads" (Psalm 22:7).	Matthew 27:39–42
"He trusts in the LORD, …let the LORD rescue him. Let him deliver him, since he delights in him" (Psalm 22:8).	Matthew 27:43–44
"And I will remove the sin of this land in a single day" (Zechariah 3:9d).	John 19:33
"Strike the shepherd, and the sheep will be scattered" (Zechariah 13:7c).	Matthew 26:56; Mark 14:49–50
"I told them, 'If you think it best, give me my pay; but if not, keep it.' So they paid me thirty pieces of silver" (Zechariah 11:12).	Matthew 26:14–15

"And the LORD said to me, 'Throw it to the potter'—the handsome price at which they priced me! So I took the thirty pieces of silver and threw them into the house of the LORD to the potter" (Zechariah 11:13).	Matthew 27:3–7
"And he was numbered with the transgressors" (Isaiah 53:12d).	Mark 15:27; Matthew 27:38

Jesus Himself told the disciples about His upcoming death three times. The last time, He said,

> *We are going up to Jerusalem, and everything that is written by the prophets about the Son of Man will be fulfilled. He will be handed over to the Gentiles. They will mock him, insult him, spit on him, flog him and kill him.*
>
> **Luke 18:31–32**
> **(Emphasis added by the author)**

The book of Isaiah is known as the gospel of the Old Testament. Around 700 BC, the prophet professed the following by the power of the Holy Spirit:

1. That Jesus Christ would be born of a virgin.
2. That He would preach the good news not only to the lost sheep of Israel but also to the Gentiles and be a light to the ends of the earth.
3. That He would take upon Himself all our iniquities, even though He was sinless.
4. That by His wounds, we would be healed.
5. That kings and rulers would interrogate the Son of God, yet He would not utter a word and would stand before them silent, like a lamb waiting to be slaughtered.
6. That the righteous one would die for the unrighteous, but

He would rise from the dead.
7. That He would come again.
8. And that there would be a new heaven and new Earth (65:17–18, 66:22); New Jerusalem (as the Lord revealed to the apostle John in Revelation 21:1–2).

This is a must-read book; I encourage everyone to read at least the fifty-third chapter. I'm sure any hard hearts will be softened. May the Lord God touch your heart.

The Last Seven Words of Jesus from the Cross

1. "Father, Forgive Them, for They Do Not Know What They Do" (Luke 23:34, NKJV).

Just for a moment, try to imagine yourself hanging on a cross in the midst of indescribably painful suffering and humiliation but still having the welfare of others in mind. Our Lord Jesus was concerned not only with the salvation of those surrounding Him but also the salvation of the very ones who hammered the nails into His hands and feet. The prayer that He uttered on the cross truly revealed the depth of His love and concern for the people.

As I read the above portion on July 22, 2015, God put the thought in my heart that Jesus set a perfect example for all Christians. We, too, should prepare our minds and hearts to face the enemies, even martyrdom. The Holy Spirit reminded me of those courageous young men in Egypt who bowed down their heads to their enemies to be slaughtered because of their faith in Jesus Christ, that they, too, must have said the same prayer as our Lord did. Lately, my prayer for those enemies has been, "Father, blind their external eyes but open their spiritual (inner) eyes. Reveal to them who You are and guide them to receive Jesus as their personal Savior and friend, for they live in darkness and are deceiving many innocent souls."

2. "ASSUREDLY, I SAY TO YOU, TODAY YOU WILL BE WITH ME IN PARADISE" (LUKE 23:43, NKJV).

This was Jesus' promise of salvation to the thief who requested Him, "Lord, remember me when You come into Your kingdom" (Luke 23:42, NKJV). How awesome that was. What more can a man hope for? A thief, hanging on the cross next to the Lord, considered unworthy to live in this world and given the death penalty, acknowledged Jesus as God and repented of his sins at the very last moment. That decision changed his future forever, for now his eternity would be spent in heaven—unlike the other thief. This is true saving grace—the undeserved, unmerited favor of God!

3. "WOMAN, BEHOLD YOUR SON!" AND TO THE DISCIPLE, "BEHOLD YOUR MOTHER!" (JOHN 19:26-27A, NKJV).

Jesus' mother was full of sorrow and agony. Imagine; she wasn't able to hold her Son's hands to comfort Him, to place a kiss on His forehead, or even to wet His dry lips and mouth with a drop of water. Instead, she had to stand there, helplessly watching her Son's unbearable suffering. Only by the Father's divine grace sustaining her could Mary have survived all without having a heart attack or a nervous breakdown. Simeon's prophecy was fulfilled here, "Yes, a sword will pierce through your own soul also" (Luke 2:35a, NKJV). Although in today's society, it would be considered disrespectful to call your mother "Woman," in those days, it was a sign of great respect. When Jesus saw His beloved mother standing at the cross next to John, the disciple, He called out and told her to accept John as her son, and then He told His disciple to accept her as his mother. "And from that hour that disciple took her to his own home" (John 19:27b, NKJV). This is a lesson for the world to learn: that every adult child has the responsibility to meet the needs of their parents.

4. "ELOI, ELOI, LAMA SABACHTHANI?"—WHICH MEANS, "MY GOD, MY GOD, WHY HAVE YOU FORSAKEN ME?" (MATTHEW 27:46; MARK 15:34).

Just imagine the cry of a toddler when a child misses his or her mother. It would be unstoppable because the child developed such a bond of security and love with the mother. During Jesus' ministry, He and the Father had constant communication. Jesus told His disciples that He was in the Father, and the Father was in Him; in fact, the Father was doing His work through His Son, Jesus (John 14:10). They were inseparable. Here, the Son of God was in deep anguish when He felt the separation from His Father at the very crucial time of His earthly life (mission), as He took upon Himself the world's sin. Most likely, the Father didn't want to be with the Son during that time; if He did, He too would have been carrying the world's sin, and that was not the Father's plan! Or probably the Father couldn't bear watching the Son carrying sins. Miraculously, darkness came upon the earth from the sixth hour until the ninth hour (Matthew 27:45), which means from 12 noon until 3 p.m., and this probably frightened His enemies, causing them to be quiet. During that same period, everyone heard Jesus' deepest cry with His last ounce of strength, "My God, my God, why have you forsaken me?" Thus, David's prophecy in Psalm 22:1 was also fulfilled.

5. "I THIRST!" (JOHN 19:28, NKJV).

This showed His true humanity. Remember, the Lord had His

last meal with the disciples on Thursday evening; since then, who knows if anyone had offered Him a glass of plain water? The Bible says He was given "wine mixed with myrrh," but He declined it (Mark 15:23). After taking up all the torture from His enemies, by Friday, close to three in the afternoon, His physical strength was completely gone, and His lips, tongue, and mouth were parched; thus, fulfilled what was foretold about the Messiah, "My strength is dried up like a potsherd, And My tongue clings to My jaws" (Psalm 22:15, NKJV). Instead of plain water, He was given "wine vinegar" (John 19:29).

6. "IT IS FINISHED!" "AND BOWING HIS HEAD, GAVE UP HIS SPIRIT" (JOHN 19:30, NKJV).

The name "Jesus" means, "He will save his people from their sins" (Matthew 1:21). Our Savior, the sinless Man-God, bore all our sins upon Himself. In our place, He was hanged on the cross, where He shed His blood, paid a full ransom for the penalty of our sins, and brought us back (reconciled us) unto the Father (Romans 5:10). Thereby, the work of salvation was completed. In other words, His redemptive work was finished according to Father's will.

7. "FATHER, 'INTO YOUR HANDS I COMMIT MY SPIRIT'" (LUKE 23:46, NKJV).

He said this as He took His last breath at 3 p.m., and the prophecy about Jesus in Psalm 31:5 was fulfilled.

After writing the above, I started praying like this, "Father, take my spirit unto Thy hands whenever, wherever, or however I die; I only want to be with You. Please forgive my sins and do not forsake me." For I don't know what state of mind I will be in at the time of my death or if I will be capable of praying at that moment.

THE CRUCIFIXION

Please consider praying in this manner as well so that you have peace of mind, knowing that you will be in heaven.

To ensure the criminals were dead before they were taken down from their crosses, the soldiers would break their legs so that they would die faster; but when they came to Jesus, they found that He had already died, which spared them from having to break His legs; thus was fulfilled the prophecy in Psalm 34:20. Still, they pierced His side with a spear; blood and water gushed out (John 19:33–34).

Just as Jesus took His last breath, three miracles took place:
1. The curtain of the temple was torn into two, from top to bottom; under normal circumstances, it would tear from bottom to upwards.
2. There was a huge earthquake that caused the rocks to split.
3. Many holy people who were dead and buried came out of the tomb alive!

(Please read Matthew 27:50–53.)

Upon witnessing Jesus' death and the miracles, the centurion in charge of a one-hundred army and his subordinates, the Gentiles, felt guilty for what they did while they guarded Him; they were terrified and said, "Truly this was the Son of God!" (Matthew 27:54, NKJV). Whereas, the Jews, the religious leaders, those who handed Jesus over to the Gentiles to be killed, instead of repenting, hardened their hearts the more. (For your own understanding, please read Matthew 27:62–66, 28:11–15.)

Because the following day was a special Sabbath, the Jews did not want to leave the body on the cross. So, that same evening, Joseph, rich but upright in heart, from a town called Arimathea in Judea, was waiting for Messiah to come (Luke 23:50–51). He, along with Nicodemus, although they both were members of the council (Mark 15:43; John 3:1), secretly followed Jesus, for they feared their fellow men. (Please read John 3:1–21 to learn about Nicodemus and the lessons he had learned from Jesus.) After Jesus' death, they showed their bravery; Joseph took permission from Pilate, the governor, to take the body from the cross, and Nicodemus brought seventy-five pounds of myrrh and aloe. They took Jesus' body and wrapped it in strips of linen with myrrh and aloe according to the Jewish burial custom. They placed Him in a new tomb that belonged to Joseph of Arimathea himself and fulfilled what was foretold, "He was assigned a grave with the wicked, and with rich in his death" (Isaiah 53:9). Lastly, they sealed the entrance to the tomb with a huge stone. Mary Magdalene and several other women were watching all this from a distance. (Please read John 19:38–42; Mark 15:42–47; Matthew 27:57–61; Luke 23:50–55.)

CHAPTER 9:

THE RESURRECTION

Looking back to the Old Testament, in the book of Isaiah, we see that God spoke to this prophet about Christ's resurrection and ascension after His suffering and death; the Lord said, "See, my servant will act wisely; he will be raised and lifted up and highly exalted" (Isaiah 52:13). And again, we read, "After the suffering of his soul, he will see the light of life and be satisfied" (Isaiah 53:11a).

David had prophesied about the resurrection, "Because you will not abandon me to the grave, nor will you let your Holy One see decay" (Psalm 16:10). That means God the Father would not let His Son's body blend with the mud. He will bring Him out of the grave alive. Also, we read, "I will proclaim the decree of the Lord: He said to me, 'You are my Son; today I have become your Father'" (Psalm 2:7). After Jesus was raised from the dead, He defeated the devil, and on the fortieth day, He victoriously returned to His Father in heaven. God the Father exalted His Son to His right side, which was also prophesied by David, "The LORD says to my Lord: 'Sit at my right hand until I make your enemies a footstool for your feet'" (Psalm 110:1). Imagine! All of this was revealed to David almost a thousand years prior to the events taking place.

Jesus Christ Himself spoke of His resurrection quite frequently, but He spoke figuratively, so the people could not understand what He was talking about. Although at times He spoke plainly, even His own disciples were unable to comprehend it, for the meaning was hidden from them—it had not yet been revealed, for they didn't have the Holy Spirit in them. For example, on three different occasions, He told the disciples that He would suffer in the hands of the Gentiles and would be killed, but on the third day, He would rise from the dead (Mark 8:31, 10:34c; Luke 18:32–33; Matthew 16:21). Another time, He told them that for a little while they would not see Him but very shortly, they would see Him again. Jesus was actually speaking of His death, burial, and resurrection, but the disciples began talking among themselves, for they were pondering, "What in the world is the Lord trying to tell us?" He also told them, "You will weep and mourn while the world rejoices. You will grieve, but your grief will turn to joy" (John 16:20). (Please read John 16:16–22.)

On another occasion, when the Pharisees and the teachers of the Law asked Him to perform a special miracle for them so they may believe in Him, Jesus told them,

> *An evil and adulterous generation seeks after a sign, and no sign will be given to it except the sign of the prophet Jonah. For as Jonah was three days and three nights in the belly of the great fish, so will the Son of Man be three days and three nights in the heart of the earth.*
>
> **Matthew 12:39–40 (NKJV)**
> **(Emphasis added by the author)**

Who would imagine that He was speaking of His burial and His resurrection?

All four Gospels declare the resurrection of the Lord Jesus Christ. They tell how He appeared to His disciples and many others and how He also did numerous miracles proving that He had

THE RESURRECTION

resurrected from the dead. As it is written in the previous chapter, Jesus was crucified and died on a Friday, and was buried on the same day. Some of the women were witnesses to His sufferings, crucifixion, and burial, and among them, we find Mary Magdalene, from whom Jesus had removed seven demons (Mark 16:9; Luke 8:2). Once she was freed, she followed her Master everywhere, and this blessed woman was the first one to see the resurrected Christ, and even had the privilege of informing His disciples.

By reading John chapter 20, you will find that Mary Magdalene went to Jesus' tomb early Sunday morning while it was still dark. She noticed the tomb was left open, for the huge stone that sealed the entrance was removed. According to the first Gospel in the Holy Bible, "And behold, there was a great earthquake; for an angel of the Lord descended from heaven, and came and rolled back the stone from the door, and sat on it" (Matthew 28:2, NKJV). Mary noticed that her Master's body was missing! Can you imagine how you would feel if you went out to the cemetery and found your loved one's body missing from the burial space? Well, Mary Magdalene's immediate response was to run and knock at Jesus' favorite disciple's door and tell Simon Peter and John. She told them, "They have taken away the Lord out of the tomb, and we do not know where they have laid Him" (John 20:2, NKJV).

So, the disciples came running to search for the body, and they couldn't find it either. When they went into the tomb, they noticed the body was missing, but they saw the burial cloth that had been around His head, which was folded up neatly, along with some linen strips set aside separately. The disciples' spiritual eyes were still blinded from understanding the prophecies, or they could remember Jesus' teachings—that He was to rise from the dead on the third day. They went back to their own homes. However, Mary was determined not to leave the burial site unless she got an answer. She continued weeping and searching by looking into the tomb. Suddenly, she saw two angles—one sitting at the head and one at the foot of where Jesus' body had been. The following are the conversations that took place between angels and Mary, Jesus and Mary, and finally, Mary to disciples, quoted from John 20:12–18 (NKJV).

They (angels) asked Mary, "Woman, why are you weeping?"

Mary replied, "Because they have taken away my Lord, and I do not know where they have laid Him."

As she spoke this, "She turned around and saw Jesus standing there, and did not know that it was Jesus."

Then Jesus asked Mary, "Woman, why are you weeping? Whom are you seeking?"

She assumed He was a gardener and said, "Sir, if You have carried Him away, tell me where You have laid Him, and I will take Him away."

Then Jesus called her by name, "Mary!"

What an awesome moment! With great relief and tears of joy, excited, she called out in Aramaic, "Rabboni!" (which means Teacher). Although the disciples were unsuccessful in their search for Jesus, Mary, due to her amazing perseverance in following Jesus' teachings, "Ask, and it will be given to you; seek, and you will find; knock, and it will be opened to you" (Matthew 7:7, NKJV), was able to find Him when no one else could. No angel ever declared her as blessed; to me, she is….

Jesus told her, "Do not cling to Me, for I have not yet ascended to My Father; but go to My brethren and say to them, 'I am ascending to My Father and your Father, to My God and your God'" (John 20:17, NKJV).

Then Mary went to the disciples' home and declared the great news to them, "She had seen the Lord" (John 20:18, NKJV). She relayed all that Jesus had told her to tell them.

THE RESURRECTION

In the Gospel of Luke, we notice how the resurrected Christ amazed two of His disciples (not the apostles but the followers). It was on Sunday in the late afternoon, three days after Jesus' death, and they had received the report from the women that Jesus was alive and the tomb was empty. All the followers of Jesus had hoped that He would be the One to free the Israelites from Roman's bondage. In despair, two men chose to go back to Emmaus, their hometown, which was about seven miles west of Jerusalem. It must have taken a couple of hours to reach their destiny as their only means of transportation was their feet. They were somber as they walked and talked about the cruel punishment Jesus had received through their own authorities.

Suddenly, Jesus joined them, but they didn't recognize Him. They thought it was a stranger or perhaps a visitor from another country, for during Passover, people would come from all over the world. Jesus (the stranger) asked them what they were discussing as they walked. The disciples were downcast. Cleopas (one of the disciples) then responded and asked, "Are you only a visitor to Jerusalem and do not know the things that have happened here in these days?" (Luke 24:18). Jesus (the stranger) asked, "What things?" After hearing about Jesus being crucified and the women (Mary Magdalene and others, Luke 24:9–10) reporting that He is alive, Jesus (the stranger) began to explain all the Scriptures that pertained to Himself, and it must be fulfilled. From Moses through all other prophets, how Christ had to suffer that He may be glorified. As they were listening to those Scriptures, the Spirit of God began to work within them, for the Bible says, "Their hearts were burning" (Luke 24:32).

They reached their destination by evening, and Jesus (the stranger) pretended to be going farther, but the disciples encouraged Him to spend the night with them, which He accepted. As the evening meal was served, Jesus (the stranger) took the bread, prayed, broke it, and gave it to the disciples; then, their eyes were opened, and they recognized it was Jesus. Suddenly, He disappeared from their sight.

The disciples were no longer filled with despair but filled with joy and gladness. They had to proclaim their encounter with the resurrected Christ to other disciples. They walked back that same evening seven miles to Jerusalem. As they reported, Jesus came and stood among them. (Please read Luke 24:13–36.) What a joyful day!

It seems they were very closely knitted with the apostles and other followers of Jesus Christ (verse 9), for they addressed them as "some of our women, and some of our companions" (verses 22, 24). I sense they, too, were the partakers of the Last Supper and witnessed the breaking of the bread, for when Jesus broke the bread in their house, their spiritual eyes were opened. The upper room where Jesus had His Last Supper was large enough for 120 people (Acts 1:13, 15).

Apostle John writes about his witnessing of the resurrected Christ: that same evening (meaning, the day Mary Magdelene had reported to the disciples that she had seen the resurrected Christ), when the disciples were gathered in a locked room for being fear of Jews, "Jesus came and stood among them and said, 'Peace be with you!'" (John 20:19). That was to remind them, don't be afraid, He is with them. Then the Lord showed them the nail-marked hands and the side where He was pierced by the enemies. The disciples were exceedingly joyful, for the Lord has risen from the dead! Thus, fulfilled what Jesus has foretold to His disciples in John 16:20, 22; Mark 8, end of verse 31, chapter 10, end of verse 34; Luke 18:33; Matthew 16, end of verse 21. And fulfilled Jesus' response to the Pharisees when they asked for a miracle (Matthew 12:40).

Jesus again said to the disciples, "Peace be with you!" (John 20:21). And He breathed into them the Holy Spirit and gave them the authority to forgive others' sins. But Thomas missed all of the above blessings, for he was not with them at that time. When he heard from the others that they had seen the Lord, he said, "I will not believe it until I see the nail marks in his hands and put my finger where the nails were and put my hand into his side" (John 20:25, NCV).

On the following Sunday, when all the disciples were together in the house with locked doors, Jesus appeared to them again and said, "Peace be with you" (John 20:26d, NCV). He then said to Thomas, "Put your finger here, and look at my hands. Put your hand here in my side. Stop being an unbeliever and believe" (verse 27, NCV).

Then Thomas called out from the bottom of his heart, "My Lord and my God!" (verse 28, NCV).

Imagine how Thomas must have felt upon hearing his Master's voice. Perhaps he would have fallen, trembling, prostrate at His feet. Maybe he felt humbled, ashamed, and emotionally spent, especially upon hearing Jesus repeat the very same words that he had just faithlessly said to the other disciples when they had told him that they had seen the Lord and received the blessings (for better understanding, please read John 20:19–29).

I'm sure that I would have reacted in the very same manner, for if, after all the years that we had been together, you had seen something that I had not seen, I would be thinking, "Well, if you got to see, then I too want to see!" In fact, if I couldn't receive that same joy and blessing that you had received (John 20:21–23), I would probably feel left out. All that Thomas went through brought him to the place where his faith was at its highest point. He was able to acknowledge Jesus as his Lord and his God. Praise the Lord! Jesus also told Thomas that he believed because he had seen Him, but those who believe and have not seen are the ones who are blessed (John 20:29). After that, slightly over five hundred people had the privilege of seeing the resurrected Christ (1 Corinthians 15:6). The Lord had set this situation, for He was not only speaking of the believers of those days who didn't have that opportunity—He was also speaking of people like us, the future generations, who, although we have not seen, choose to believe because God the Father enabled us (John 6:65). John chapter twenty-one continues to speak about the works of the resurrected Christ. All the Gospels writers have mentioned the resurrection and what Jesus had commissioned them (please read Matthew chapter 28; Mark 16; Luke 24:1–49; Acts 1:1–9). And 1 Peter 3:18–20; 4:5–6 explains that the resurrected Christ preached the gospel to the departed souls of the Old Testament time up until the day of His resurrection. Thus making them accountable to stand on judgment day.

As I wrote this, God put the thought in my heart: Oh, what a blessed day that will be! We will see all the generations—Adam and Eve, Noah, Abraham, Isaac, Jacob, the twelve patriarchs, Moses, David, Elijah, Elisha, Isaiah, all the prophets, Mother Mary, the righteous Joseph, John the Baptist, Mary Magdalene, all the apostles and saints, our grandparents, parents, siblings, friends, relatives, spouses, children, and the generations to come. I cannot wait for that awesome day. I pray that my name will be found in the Book of Life when the Lord opens it on judgment day. Please read Revelation 3:5, 20:11–15, 21:27, to learn about the uniqueness of this "Lamb's Book of Life." And you might want to pray that your name also will be recorded in the Book of Life so that you can spend your eternity with Jesus!

Let us now go to the first book in the Old Testament, where God proclaimed to Satan, "And I will put enmity between you and the woman, and between your offspring and hers; he will crush your head, and you will strike his heel" (Genesis 3:15). From the time of the fall of man, God the Father's plan was to defeat Satan by sending His Son to be born of a virgin, live a sinless life, bear our sins upon Him, die on the cross, raise from the dead on the third day, and be exalted to the Father's right side, thus crushing the head of Satan. Although Satan had tried his best to test and challenge the Son of God, *Jesus became victorious in accomplishing His mission according to Father's plans and will.*

Now, Jesus' crucifixion, death, and resurrection gave me a greater understanding of His spoken words,

> *And as Moses lifted up the serpent in the wilderness, even so must the Son of Man be lifted up, that whoever believes in Him should not perish but have eternal life. For God so loved the world that He gave His only begotten Son, that whoever believes in Him should not perish but have everlasting life.*
>
> **John 3:14–16 (NKJV)**
> **(Emphasis added by the author)**

Just as God commanded, Moses lifted up the bronze snake on a pole in the desert, and those who looked at the elevated snake survived the poisonous snakebite (please read Numbers 21:4–9). This was the foreshadowing of Jesus' crucifixion; if we would look up to Jesus Christ and believe that He was lifted up on the cross, died there for our sins, was resurrected on the third day, and ascended into heaven, then we will never die spiritually but have everlasting life.

On December 26, 2015, I was confused; I didn't think it was important to write the above information, so I deleted it. Then I felt I was doing something wrong, so I clicked on "undo" and brought it back. That same evening, while I was on the treadmill, I turned on the television to TBN. Dr. Charles Stanly was speaking about the importance of Christmas, and he used these same verses (John 3:14–16) and said, "These two are the most important message of Christmas." When I heard this, I was amazed, for prior to this, I had heard priests using these verses for delivering the Easter message, but never for Christmas. This is how sometimes God gives me confirmation. Again, on May 1, 2016, at 7:15 a.m. (after Easter), I heard the message on the same verses over the radio. Thank You, Holy Spirit, for Your guidance in writing all throughout this (Your) book. After all these, my heart said, look at the notes God the Father had given me on the day of the vision, and I did. Surely, there it was!

My beloved reader, I pray that God the Father gives you the wisdom to choose what is right—and that is to receive Jesus Christ in your heart as your Lord and Savior, for there is no other God like He who laid down His life for the sins of the world and yet lives forever. Had not Jesus risen from the dead, there would have been no Christianity. He still is in control of everything! Amen.

CHAPTER 10:

WHO AM I, OH LORD, THAT YOU HAVE BROUGHT ME SO FAR?

As I was writing the history of the Passover, I thought of how merciful God was to the Israelites. I cried when I thought of my journey and how God has been with me all the way. I asked, "Who am I, oh Lord, that You would bring me this far?"

I was born in a rural village in the southern part of India during World War II (at a time when the world was suffering financially, including our family, to the point of food rationing). Eventually, it even became difficult just to put food on the table. The particular area where we lived could not receive electricity, and even if it had been available, we couldn't have afforded it. But we never let it discourage us. Thanks to our kerosene lamps, we had enough light to complete our homework and join together morning and evening for our family devotions, singing, Bible reading, and prayer.

While I was in high school, I found myself dreaming of becoming a nurse. I visualized myself wearing the white uniform, the nurse's hat, and even the little gold-framed eyeglasses. Until I made my first trip to Bombay, the largest city in India, I actually had no shoes—not even a pair of sandals—although it may sound as if we were homeless, we did have a small, old-fashioned wooden house (*arrayum nirayum*), some land, and a rice paddy. There were those times when the fruits of our labors were washed away by a flood or destroyed by drought. I'm sure my parents must have been heartbroken quite often, yet God held all eight of us together.

There was always a lot of love and joy in our home, even though there were constant financial struggles. Whenever there was a quarrel between the siblings, for sure, that evening, my father would make us stand in line, from the oldest to the youngest, while he preached the entire Psalm 133; I would quote only the first verse, "BEHOLD, how good and how pleasant it is For brethren to dwell together in unity!" (NKJV). Please read the rest of this psalm; it is awesome for every family, whether they are blood or spiritual relations.

Achieving my dream of nursing started to materialize when I received admission to one of the most famous hospitals in all of India, and it happened to be in Bombay, a thousand miles away from home. After going with me to enroll in the J. J. Group of Hospitals' School of Nursing, my father, Mathai Mathias, I called him "Achan," returned home and seemed to be very depressed, not eating or drinking and hardly speaking due to the fact that his daughter had surprised and disappointed him. She had decided to become a nurse instead of the teacher he wanted her to be; even today, nursing is still not considered a dignified profession in my culture. Thank God that after a period of time, Achan changed his mind and became proud of his daughter.

During my younger years, I never imagined going to America, but in 1972, guess what? It happened! In the late nineteen sixties, during President Nixon's time, America began recruiting nursing professionals from foreign countries, including India, and I was one among them. What a blessing! I found myself in the world's biggest city, New York. It was there, for the first time in my life, I saw a television screen.

After living urban life for nearly two years, I started thinking it was time for me to begin considering marriage, so I returned home. While there, I received approximately one hundred marriage proposals from young men, almost all of whom were just too young. I was determined to marry a man who was at least one year older than me. Most of these men seemed to be seeking a free ticket to America and a better way of life; I simply wasn't interested in any of them.

Then I met Simon. He was tall, handsome, quite a bit older, and from a very distinguished and highly influential family. Not many young Indian girls in the nursing profession or from lower middle-class families would have ever dreamed of such an opportunity. Even though Simon's motive for coming to our home that day with his older sister was the same as that of all the other young men, I was glad that I found an older person as I had desired. I came to realize later in life that this was all part of God's divine appointment for our lives. After we had been married for a little less than a month, I returned to the United States, and two months later, Simon joined me, the city known as the "city that never sleeps" and the "home of the Yankees."

In the years to come, even with my language barrier, I worked in various departments of nursing, several times in management, and at least once in an administrative position. At last, after thirty-five years, my retirement arrived. Simon had already retired, and we had no idea where we wanted to settle. We had heard over the years that Florida was a good place for retirees, and we knew of one couple that went to Georgia upon their retirement, so I prayed about where we should go. Soon, the Lord gave me His answer, and it was Georgia. This was a place where we had no family or friends—we would be total strangers, except for the one couple that we knew, but even they decided to move to Florida less than a year after my husband moved to Georgia. Believe it or not, the Lord already had built the house for us according to the desire of my heart; He is amazing! I knew that with God, as Frank Sinatra sang, if we could make it in New York, we could make it anywhere.

I truly began growing in my relationship with the Lord Jesus Christ in 2003, after God the Father sent me a message through the prophetess Norma Perez. After a truly wonderful and informative conversation with her, I took her advice. I spent more and more time studying the Scriptures. Soon, I began hearing Him speak to me.

For several years before I retired, I prayed that once I stopped working, the Lord would help me to completely surrender myself to Him and that He would use me as His servant for the rest of my life. Over the years, I learned the true meaning of the Scripture found in Matthew 9:37–38, when Jesus said to His disciples, "The harvest is plentiful but the workers are few. Ask the Lord of the harvest, therefore, to send out workers into his harvest field." So I prayed to God, "Here I am, Lord. Please, use me as Your servant."

God's timing is so perfect! I retired in September 2007 and also graduated from the New York School of the Bible at the same time with an advanced certificate. I thank God Almighty for guiding me throughout my life and quenching my thirst for the living Word of God. It seems I couldn't get enough of God's words. The more I study, the more I want to know; the closer I feel to Him, the more my faith grows. It has come to the point where I realize that I am nothing and He is everything. I can't do—and don't want to do—*anything* without Him. If it weren't for the New York School of the Bible and its faculty, today, ten years later, I would still be struggling to know what the Bible is really all about.

Going to school after work wasn't as easy as one would think. Regardless of the weather (rain, shine, or snow), I rode the bus or subway from my work to the Bible school. Late at night, I was once again riding the subway and Long Island Railroad back to the home station, where I would either call my husband to pick me up or take a cab to the house. I went through all this because my soul was craving its spiritual food. Just as our body needs physical food, our soul needs spiritual food (the Word of God) to survive. Since I wanted to have the most personal relationship with my Lord Jesus Christ that I could ever have, as well as defend my faith, I was willing to do whatever it took to obtain the deepest understanding of the Word of God. Jesus said,

> *I am the vine; you are the branches. If a man remains in me and I in him, he will bear much fruit; apart from me you can do nothing. If anyone does not remain in me, he is like a branch that is thrown away and withers; such branches are picked up, thrown into the fire and burned. If you remain in me and my words remain in you, ask whatever you wish, and it will be given you. This is to my Father's glory, that you bear much fruit, showing yourselves to be my disciples.*
>
> **John 15:5–8**
> **(Emphasis added by the author)**

I just want to be a productive servant of my Lord Jesus Christ.

God is so amazing; He already had work lined up for me even before I left New York. As soon as I arrived in my new home, Father Mathew Koshy, the vicar of the St. Thomas Orthodox Church Atlanta, visited us as part of his routine to welcome the newcomers. He knew what an active participant I was in my previous parish, and he asked me to lead the women's group. I jumped at the opportunity, for my desire was to teach the women the Bible. In early 2008, I began to take classes every Sunday after the holy service. The ladies, young and old alike, were very eager and joyful to study the Scriptures verse by verse. I could see their hunger and thirst for the living Word of God!

Also, the Lord blessed me with several wonderful women's Bible studies in our community, such as those from Beth Moore, Kay Arthur, and Priscilla Shirer—these studies strengthened me spiritually. In fact, in 2010, I was tremendously blessed to have the opportunity to personally attend their conference in Birmingham, Alabama, and I thank Liz Martinez, the Bible class leader, for her kindness in taking me.

In 2008, I began compiling data from the Holy Bible to write this book; it took me almost a year. My one and only tool was the New International Life Application Study Bible; its concordances, references, footnotes, or commentaries, maps, and the introduction of each book, most importantly, the dates of events, for I chose to use the dates from this Bible to indicate the dates of events (occurrences) in this book. The commentaries gave me a better understanding of the Scriptures, as well as the confirmation. After learning the computer from my daughter, Maureen, using two or three fingers, I began inputting all the material the Lord had given me. This took another eight or nine months to complete.

During this time, I was constantly praying and crying out to God, "Lord, You know that I am not capable of writing this book. I can't publish Your book without a writer, one who knows the Bible very well and also has complete faith in You."

Our wonderful God is so compassionate. He heard my cry, and within a year, He answered my prayer. My precious husband knew the burden I had been carrying, for in the mornings and evenings, when we prayed together, he would hear me cry out to God for help. One day, we were watching the news at noon, and a newscaster reported that a large company had hired a writer to sell their products. I started telling my husband, "See, even the big companies are hiring writers; I need one too." I had never heard of such a report ever before or thereafter.

So Simon himself began helping me by googling "biblical book writer." During his search, he found a website called FaithWriters. As soon as he saw the long list of biblical book writers whose names were posted on the site, he hollered, "Leela, I've found something; I think you need to come and take a look."

I dropped what I was doing and rushed upstairs to see what my husband was so excited about. As soon as I saw the long list of writers' names, I immediately thanked God for this awesome revelation, and I began going through each person's profile.

I checked the files daily; each day, some new names were added, and others were deleted. I looked at information on so many people; some even fit the criteria I was looking for, but I was totally surprised when I realized that most were from so far away. There were some from Texas, California, and many other states. It was important to me to work closely with this person so that they understood that God Himself was the author of this book. I was merely the instrument that He chose to get His message out to the world. I felt it would be much better to continue my search until I found someone close enough to work with one-on-one on a regular basis. We needed to work on the manuscript together, for I had to be certain that they did not alter God's Word by adding their own thoughts, ideas, or frills to His message. Simon and I continued our search until, at last, Simon found a person in Georgia, the very criteria that I was looking for: Carolyn Weeks May. She was the only one from Georgia; we later found that she lived less than six miles from our home. What a mighty God!

When I called the number listed in her profile, a gentleman answered the phone and said, "She's retired and no longer working here."

In my desperation, I asked him, "How can I reach her?"

He asked me, "What is this in reference to?"

I told him I needed help writing a Christian book, and he immediately gave me her home number. Later on, I found out that he was the writer's son. I called several times and left her messages via voicemail, but I never received a return phone call. I called once more, and finally, Carolyn answered, and we made an appointment to meet. She said, "Every Friday evening, we have dinner and a prayer meeting. Why don't you and your husband come this Friday at 6 p.m.?"

So, on Friday, February 4, 2010, Simon and I went to her house and attended the prayer meeting; Carolyn served us dinner. Later that same evening, I showed her the article I had typed. While she was reading, I was praying, "Lord, please make her say yes." And as soon as she read "The Vision," she said, "I'll gladly help you." Instantly, all my stress and tension were gone—I was filled with joy and thanked God, for from the very first time we spoke on the phone, I had been praying that she wouldn't turn me down.

Before leaving Carolyn's house that night, we set an appointment to get together again and start writing. On our trip home, Simon and I wondered whether she would actually be capable of writing the book—especially when we had both witnessed Carolyn dozing off at dinner, with her face almost in the soup bowl. After all, she had told us that she had been diagnosed with Parkinson's disease, and the medications had some very adverse side effects. But we decided to give it a try, and once we began working together, and I saw how she formulated the sentences and inputted them into the computer so rapidly, I became excited about her work.

I asked her, "What do you want in return for what you're doing?"

Carolyn replied, "I wouldn't take any money for helping you write this book because I feel it is such a privilege to serve the Lord. Besides, when He calls you to write something for His glory, you are simply the fifty-nine-cent ballpoint pen He holds in His hand—He is actually the Author."

I was in shock. I couldn't think of what to say. On my way back home, I kept thinking. When I reached home, I discussed with my husband how to pay Carolyn for her work, but Simon and I couldn't come up with a concrete decision.

The next time Carolyn and I got together, I told her, "I don't want you to work free of charge because I don't want to take credit for what I have not done." I insisted that Carolyn be the coauthor of this book.

She responded, "I'm only taking what you give me and writing, rearranging the sentences, or correcting the grammar."

I said to her, "I could never write like that, so your name will go in the book as assisted by."

She replied, "Do whatever the Lord lays on your heart."

Not long after we began writing on a regular basis, Carolyn started asking me how I found her. She couldn't believe it when I told her I found her on the FaithWriters website. She was shocked, for she said she had discontinued her membership and taken her name and work off that website. She had not paid dues for two years. Even today, four years later, we are still talking about the fact that it had to be a "God thing." Our relationship not only wrote this book, but it also gave me the opportunity to reach out to the lost in prisons and jails with Bill Glass of Champions for Life Ministries. I have been so blessed to have been used by God to lead some of these precious ladies to a saving knowledge of the Lord Jesus Christ, give some the assurance of their salvation, and help others rededicate their lives to the Lord.

Another thrilling event that took place in my life was one that occurred on my second prison weekend, and that was when Carolyn introduced me to Bill Glass. He was not only the founder and head of Champions for Life Ministries but also a former professional, award-winning football player for the Cleveland Browns. Despite all his success and popularity, in 1972 (the year I came to America), Bill humbled himself and chose to set it all aside in order to serve his Lord and Savior full-time, going into prisons all across America and many foreign countries.

As time progressed, I became more and more excited about teaching the Bible. When Carolyn asked me to teach an adult class at her home each week, I jumped at the chance. I felt so blessed to be helping men and women grow in their relationship with the Lord. At about that same time, I became involved in several prayer chains at various hours of the day and night. We have seen some huge answers to prayer. I stand amazed the Lord has chosen me as His servant in all of these areas.

There is one incident that will always stand out to me; I thank God for the opportunity He gave me to minister to a brilliant young man named Stephen. The first time Stephen attended the Friday night Bible study I was teaching, I knew immediately that he was not only extremely intelligent but was also an accomplished orator. When he first arrived, he let it be known that he spent a lot of time studying the Bible. Due to his exceptional communication skills, I felt a little bit intimidated, wondering how I would be able to minister to him most effectively with the language barrier that existed between us. I began praying that God would fill everyone at the table with the Holy Spirit so that at the end of the evening, each person would have a total understanding of the Scriptures that had been covered. As for me, I wanted my teaching to be completely controlled by the Holy Spirit so that I wouldn't be anxious and fearful about teaching with this young man present. The Lord graciously answered my prayer, and several times during the study, Stephen excitedly made the comment that he had never heard many of the things I was saying. He even said he had never heard anyone teach like that before and knew he was hearing the truth. Praise be to God!

Now, for about two years, Carolyn, the mother of the prisons, and I had been longing and praying for the opportunity to teach a weekly Bible study at one of our local facilities. We were absolutely amazed when we heard we had been approved to go into one of the men's units every Wednesday. We held our first class on November 6, 2012, with six men in attendance. The numbers kept growing every week, and by April 24, 2013, there were about thirty men attending the class. It has been such a joy and privilege for me to take the Word of God to these men and see the Lord use His words to transform their lives. Prisons are the last place most people would visualize God because they think the inmates inhabiting those facilities are evildoers and deserve what they get. Little do they realize that these people are the very ones who know they need a Savior, and they are so appreciative when someone takes the time to go into the prisons and share Christ with them. They are very grateful that there are others who truly care for their souls. As Christians, we should always be ready to go wherever the Lord leads us to take the gospel.

There is one thing I now know for sure, and that is that God was in that remote village called Pampady, in Kerala State, where I was born. He has been with me from the very beginning, guiding and directing my life. He will be with me all the way to the end. This very God was the same with the Israelites as He has been with me; He will also be with you. He is the same yesterday, today, and forever (Hebrews 13:8). We must all remember to give God the glory, the praise, and the credit for all He does in our lives. We must quit trying to take credit for it ourselves. The wisdom book teaches us, "Trust in the LORD with all your heart and lean not on your own understanding; in all your ways acknowledge him, and he will make your paths straight" (Proverbs 3:5–6).

As I was writing this book, I couldn't help comparing my life with that of the Israelites, and it often made me cry, for it brought thoughts to my heart that compelled me to write about the path my life had taken. I truly felt the Lord urging me to include this information in the book; He plainly let me know that without it, this book would not be complete. Just as the Israelites were brought from slavery to Canaan, where milk and honey were flowing, God brought me from the poorest of the poorest countries to the richest country on Earth, where milk and honey are flowing. I often wonder what my life would have been like had I not asked God's direction and obeyed Him in retiring to Georgia rather than going to Florida and listening to my own will.

My advice to all the readers of this book is that you should not do anything according to your own will; instead, submit your request to the Lord and pray about it. You may have major issues, concerns, or changes that need to be made in your life, or you may be in doubt about something; simply ask Him, seek Him, and knock at His door. God is omnipresent (present everywhere at the same time), omniscient (all-knowing), and omnipotent (all-powerful). Because of His attributes, we can communicate with Him anytime, day and night, and anyplace: traveling by land, sea, or air, even on the moon or Mars, walking in the park, at the workplace or at school, in the playground, when taking a shower, cooking in the kitchen, washing the dishes, or anywhere else, and there is no need to make an appointment. He is a "Wonderful Counselor, Mighty God, Everlasting Father, Prince of Peace" (Isaiah 9:6b). Yet, His advice comes to you at no cost, and there is but one criterion: take the advice and be obedient to it.

Why God Had to Come Down; and the Authenticity of the Bible

As I was to complete this book (in the late spring of 2016), I had an encounter with a young man who claimed to be a Christian but didn't believe the Bible was God's written Word.

He said, "God did not write the Bible; some men did." He also said other things I choose not to disclose.

He asked, "Why did God have to come all the way from heaven to die for me, and now I have to die for Him?"

My heart was troubled, but I replied, "You need not die for Him; He has already died for you. Do you have Holy Spirit in you?"

He answered, "No."

My heart burned like fire as I asked him, "How are you able to raise your children?" (Since he had two and the younger one was present at the time of the discussion.)

He answered, "They will believe whatever they choose."

He walked away, leaving me a little concerned. From that day forth, I began praying for him like this, "Father, please remove the evil spirit from this young man; give him wisdom, knowledge, and understanding of the Scriptures. Fill him with Your Spirit."

A couple of months later, the Lord reminded me of the question the young man had asked me—why did God have to come all the way from heaven and die for him, and now he has to die for Him? The Holy Spirit then laid on my heart, "A blind person cannot lead another blind person. In a like manner, a sinner cannot save another sinner."

There is not a single person without sin, "For all have sinned and fall short of the glory of God" (Romans 3:23). God's Spirit revealed to me an awesome message in the Old Testament, "No man can redeem the life of another or give to God a ransom for him—the ransom for life is costly, no payment is ever enough" (Psalm 49:7-8) I was astounded! Who can fathom the value of Jesus' blood that was shed on the cross for our salvation? So, God, who never sins, came down from the most-high position to die once for the sins of all generations. Whether past, present, or future—from Adam to the end of ages, He descended from heaven to die for us!

I had no desire to mention the above conversation in this book, but when the Holy Spirit gave me the marvelous answers to the young man's question, I felt compelled to do so.

THE AUTHENTICITY OF THE BIBLE

It was God who engraved the ten commandments on two stone tablets (Exodus 24:12, 31:18, 32:15–16; Deuteronomy 10:3–4); therefore, it was God Himself who started to write the Bible. The Lord wrote not with paper and pen, but He inscribed with His mighty, powerful finger!

The word "Bible" is derived from the Greek word "*Biblia*," which means a collection of books; there are sixty-six books in the Bible. God chose forty men—thirty-nine of them were Jews and one Gentile, Luke—to write down His instructions for the whole world (the Bible says He breathed out into them), which would lead us to the right path. Apostle Paul wrote, "All Scripture is God-breathed and is useful for teaching, rebuking, correcting and training in righteousness, so that the man of God may be thoroughly equipped for every good work" (2 Timothy 3:16–17). (I learned all these from the Bible school.) Unless God guided those men to write down His words, there would have been no Bible, for no human mind can ever imagine or think so high as God. The Lord declared, "As the heavens are higher than the earth, so are my ways higher than yours and my thoughts than your thoughts" (Isaiah 55:9). Apostle Peter explains,

> *Above all, you must understand that no prophecy of Scripture came about by the prophet's own interpretation. For prophecy never had its origin in the will of man, but men spoke from God as they were carried*

along by the Holy Spirit.

**2 Peter 1:20–21
(Emphasis added by the author)**

Even in this book I am writing, unless the Lord had been my guide, teacher, and instructor, I would have never ever come up with such an idea or thought.

God Raises the Poor from the Dust

"He raises the poor from the dust and lifts the needy from the ash heap; he seats them with princes, with the princes of their people" (Psalm 113:7–8). As I was reading these verses on September 19, 2009, I compared them to myself and said to God, "It is like me, O Lord," for the Lord brought me out of poverty to where milk and honey were flowing, and He made me marry the man who is from a very prominent family, of which I was not worthy.

Again, when I read the same verses on December 12, 2012, the Lord put different thoughts in my heart, "This is exactly like President Obama and First Lady Michelle Obama, for their ancestors were slaves." I watched them visiting the queen of England, Elizabeth II, on television, and as they were welcomed by the queen into the highness' royal palace, the Lord reminded me of the above verses, and I was very joyful, for knowing how God had lifted them up to be seated with the princess (the queen)!

The Lord had been putting the thought in my heart to write about them for the past few years, but I had been putting it off. Lately, God has been compelling me to write; today (January 14, 2017) is the day I finally wrote about how God elevated this couple!

Michelle's great-great-grandfather was a slave, according to Wikipedia, and how blessed is her mother, the great-granddaughter of a slave! She lived in the White House for eight years with her first and second generations, and she ate at the same table with the president of the United States of America! Who can fathom the Almighty's plans for each one of us and the generations to come?

I was very emotional and was crying as I wrote the above article. Then the Holy Spirit put the thought in my heart, "Every word in the Bible is true!" If we study the Scriptures with all our heart, paying attention to every word, the Holy Spirit will reveal to us its hidden meanings. Only then will we have the ability to observe and admire how God's words are being fulfilled every day of our lives.

A year also later, as I waited for the Lord to guide me to a traditional publishing house, the Holy Spirit put the thought in my heart about Hadassah, also known as Esther. A young, beautiful Jewish girl who lost both her parents was adopted by her fraternal cousin, Mordecai, and he brought her up as his own daughter. It seems she was very obedient to her cousin, for whatever he instructed her to do, she did it. They were the descendants of those exiled from Judah to Babylon; they kept the Jewish customs. Instead of returning to their own country, Judah, they chose to live in Susa, the capital city of Persia. The king of Persia, Xerxes/Ahasuerus, was very rich and treated his officials lavishly.

Unfortunately, or otherwise, Queen Vashti, his wife, was disrespectful to her husband, causing the king to put her away and search for another queen. His empire was extremely large, starting from the border of Bharath (India) to the border of Cush (Ethiopia) with 127 provinces. The king sent out a decree to bring in all the young, beautiful virgins from every province to the palace, where they would get beauty treatment for a year. It seems like a national beauty pageant competition! Although the king was a Gentile, Mordecai, the Jew, couldn't resist the opportunity to send his cousin Esther with the instruction not to disclose her ethnicity.

After a year of beauty treatment, the time had come to choose the most beautiful young virgin. Guess who was the most favorable one? The orphan, Esther! Thus, she became the queen. I wonder, if her parents were alive, would history have been made? Although Esther lived in the palace, her cousin was in constant correspondence with her, informing her of all the news that happened outside of the royal palace. There came a gravest situation for all the Jews living in that kingdom because of one man, Haman, the noble of King Xerxes. He made a plot against Mordecai, for he refused to kneel and honor him. So, Haman influenced the king to send out a decree to kill all the Jews who lived in 127 provinces on a set date. Who can fathom their fear? There was great mourning and wailing; they began to fast, and many put on the sackcloth, including Mordecai, and laid in ashes.

Mordecai urged Queen Esther to plead with the king to stop the annihilation of Jews even if it cost her her life going to the king at an unauthorized time. They were debating each other, but Esther couldn't resist Mordecai's faithful words, written in the book of Esther chapter four, verses twelve through fourteen. He insisted if she didn't act upon it now, the deliverance of Jews would come from some other source. Again, he encouraged her, "And who knows but that you have come to royal position for such a time as this?" (Esther 4:14). Now they were respectful of each other's advice, she instructed him what to do in the city while she was going to do something wise inside the palace. The queen was able to please the king and revoked the edit that was sent out to the whole kingdom! Not only was she able to stop the killing of the Jews, but she also announced that that set date would be a day of feast, a national holiday, "Purim." The Lord turned their "wailing into dancing," as the psalmist said in Psalm 30:11. Isn't it amazing how God lifts up the least of the least and brings glory and honor to Him through them? Even today, the Jews are celebrating this holiday every year.

As you read the entire book of "Esther," you will also learn how severely the Lord punished Haman, the wicked, and how He uplifted Mordecai, the righteous. I'm very happy to notice that "India" (Bharath), my native country, has been mentioned twice in the Holy Bible: in the book of Esther, chapter one, verse one, and chapter eight, verse nine.

CHAPTER 11:

THE GREAT DAY OF THE LORD

God is true; He speaks the truth, and He keeps His promises. "God is not a man, that he should lie, nor a son of man, that he should change his mind. Does he speak and then not act? Does he promise and not fulfill?" (Numbers 23:19). We can see God's promise, "So is my word that goes out from my mouth: It will not return to me empty, but will accomplish what I desire and achieve the purpose for which I sent it" (Isaiah 55:11). (Please, first read verse 10 for better understanding.) His words are everlasting, "The grass withers and the flowers fall, but the word of our God stands for ever" (Isaiah 40:8). In Jesus' Sermon on the Mount, He emphasized, "I tell you the truth, until heaven and earth disappear, not the smallest letter, not the least stroke of a pen, will by any means disappear from the Law until everything is accomplished" (Matthew 5:18). Jesus said, "Heaven and earth will pass away, but my words will never pass away" (Luke 21:33, Matthew 24:35, and Mark 13:31). I quoted these verses for you to understand how serious it is when it comes to either written or spoken words of God. Please do not take them easily or neglect them but revere them.

By now, we have learned that whatever God has either revealed through the prophets or spoken personally about Jesus' birth, His ministry, suffering, death, resurrection, and ascension has definitely been fulfilled. There is no doubt whatsoever that whatever is left to be fulfilled will be. There are many prophecies written in the Old Testament about the second advent of Jesus Christ, and I will give you a couple of addresses so you can read them for your own benefit. They are Zechariah 14:5–7; Daniel 12 (I encourage you to read the whole chapter, and please pay attention to verse thirteen, what an amazing promise God had made to this prophet Daniel about two thousand five hundred years ago); Isaiah 30:27–28, 63:1–4; Joel 2:10–11; and Amos 9:11–12. Before Christ came to this earth, God spoke through prophets of that which was yet to come.

But in the New Testament time, the Lord spoke through His Son, Jesus. We read,

> *In the past God spoke to our forefathers through prophets at many times and in various ways, but in these last days he has spoken to us by his Son, whom he appointed heir of all things, and through whom he made the universe.*
>
> **Hebrews 1:1–2**
> **(Emphasis added by the author)**

As you read your Bible, you will find compelling evidence supporting Christ's return; in fact, on the fortieth day after His resurrection, as the disciples eagerly watched, He ascended into heaven from the Mount of Olives. All of a sudden, two men dressed in white (the heavenly host) appeared to them and said, "Men of Galilee, …why do you stand here looking into the sky? *This same Jesus, who has been taken from you into heaven, will come back in the same way you have seen him go into heaven*" (Acts 1:11) (emphasis added by the author). (Please read Acts 1:9–11.)

Apostle Paul wrote,

> *For the Lord Himself will descend from heaven with a shout, with the voice of an archangel, and with the trumpet of God. And the dead in Christ will rise first. Then we who are alive and remain shall be caught up together with them in the clouds to meet the Lord in the air. And thus we shall always be with the Lord.* **Therefore** *comfort one another with these words.*
>
> **1 Thessalonians 4:16–18 (NKJV)**
> **(Emphasis added by the author)**

When this event takes place, the feet of Jesus will not touch the ground, but instead, every believer (both dead and alive) will be caught up together to meet the Lord in the air. We do not know when Jesus will return, and we don't want to miss this blessed occasion; therefore, we must be reminded of this event every day of our lives and be ready, also tell others.

About two thousand years ago, Jesus Himself revealed everything to His disciples, the signs of the end days—what to watch for, how cautious we must be, how He will judge us on that day when He returns, and how dreadful it will be on the day of the Lord (please read chapters Matthew 24; Mark 13; Luke 17:20–37, 21:5–36). The King specifically and repeatedly said, "See, I have told you beforehand" (Matthew 24:25, NKJV). *"But take heed; see, I have told you all things beforehand"* (Mark 13:23, NKJV) (emphasis added by the author). So, I must say, this is our preparation time. Listen to our Creator. Jesus is definitely coming back, and upon His return, He will bring salvation to those who wait on Him.

The first sign amongst the list was the destruction of the Jerusalem temple and its surrounding buildings, "Not one stone here will be left on another; every one will be thrown down" (Matthew 24:2). Which took place in AD 70; history says, the temple was completely destroyed by the Romans.

Jesus reminds us in Matthew 24:37–39 that it will be similar to the days of Noah when the people didn't believe there would ever be a flood.

> *Then the LORD saw that the wickedness of man was great in the earth, and that every intent of the thoughts of his heart was only evil continually. And the LORD was sorry that He had made man on the earth, and He was grieved in His heart.*
>
> **Genesis 6:5–6 (NKJV)**
> **(Emphasis added by the author)**

God searched the world over and found one blameless man, Noah, and thus, by His grace, did not destroy all of mankind. However, the Lord did choose to destroy the entire earth with a flood. The Lord said to Noah, "The end of all flesh has come before Me, for the earth is filled with violence through them; and behold, I will destroy them with the earth" (Genesis 6:13, NKJV). In preparation for the coming destruction, God told Noah to build an ark 450 feet long, 75 feet wide, and 45 feet high, with three decks and rooms not only for Noah and his family of eight but for the different types of animals and creatures that He had created—one pair of each, male and female (for better understanding, please read Genesis 6:14–20. In fact, the entire chapters of 6 and 7). I'm sure Noah might not have carried enough supplies to last for a year; although Earth was flooded only for forty days and forty nights, it took one whole year to recede all the water from the land; until then, they remained on the ark (Genesis 8:13–16). God must have kept on multiplying the food just as Jesus did with five loaves of bread and two fish. Is there anything impossible for God? God put these thoughts in my heart today, August 27, 2017.

Besides all these, he had to store up all kinds of food, not only for his family but for all different types of animals. (Praise the Lord!)

THE GREAT DAY OF THE LORD

Can you imagine all the time and hard labor it took in those days to build an ark (boat) that size? The Bible does not specify how many years of labor it took; surely it took many decades, if not one hundred years, for Noah was five hundred years old by the time he had three children (Genesis 5:32). And when he was six hundred years old, the rain fell, and the whole family entered the ark on that day (Genesis 7:6–7). In those days, they had no electricity and no modern tools like we have, and they had to start from scratch by cutting down the cypress trees and sawing them into boards of different shapes and sizes. This was an unbelievable assignment for Noah because he had only his wife, their three sons, and their wives as laborers. Even if he had tried to warn the people of those days, they probably could not have imagined what it meant to have a flood; after all, they had never even experienced rain. I can just picture Noah being mocked, insulted, and laughed at by his friends, neighbors, relatives, and passersby, calling him names instead of repenting of their sins and turning to God. Noah paid no attention to them and worked diligently in obedience to the Lord.

Noah had done all that God had directed him to do, and as the flood started, family members, as well as the animals, got on board, and it was the Lord Himself who closed the door of the ark (Genesis 7:16). Until that day, others were going on with their lives, violence as usual—"eating and drinking, marrying and giving in marriage" (Matthew 24:38)—but I can easily visualize the chaos the people must have been in as they ran toward the ark, and I can almost hear them shouting, "Help, help, Noah! Help, open the door, and let us in. Take us with you." But they all perished!

[It seems the clock is ticking back to Noah's time, for violence and wickedness are increasing day by day in today's world! God put this thought in my heart today, May 4, 2023.]

Just as in Noah's time, there will be no change in our lifestyle either. We will be enjoying life as usual—having fun; some will be drinking in the bar or enjoying themselves in a nightclub, some will be playing cards and gambling in casinos, and there will still be others getting married. Mothers will be feeding their children, and some will be working, some even sleeping, and others will carry out the violence. We will never know when Jesus will appear, just like we don't know when a thief will break into our house or car. It will definitely be a surprise visit, so we must be ready for it at any moment. Jesus Himself said, "Behold, I come like a thief! Blessed is he who stays awake [spiritually alert] and keeps his clothes with him, so that he may not go naked and be shamefully exposed" (Revelation 16:15).

How do we get ready? Imagine when all the people were going after worldly pleasures; Noah was found to be blameless, for he never was tempted to follow the people of his time. In fact, he fixed his eyes on God and persevered to accomplish the Lord's instructions; therefore, he and his family were saved. Likewise, we, too, must fix our eyes, minds, hearts, and souls on Jesus Christ instead of having the desire for worldly pleasures, which is the devil's decisiveness. Apostle Peter explains this so beautifully in his Epistle; please follow his teachings as well, 2 Peter 3:10–15a, 17–18. This is a perfect example that God does not look at our education, job, wealth, or family status; He only looks at our hearts: are they humble, willing, and obedient to Him? No man can comprehend godly matters unless the Lord Himself reveals it to them. Peter, in his early days, was a fisherman and unschooled, yet during his apostolic era, he was guided by the Holy Spirit, and he penned them by the power of the Holy Spirit. So, follow his teachings and trust the whole Bible. Surely then, on that Great Day of the Lord, when Jesus comes, He will take us with Him into His kingdom!

As we read further in Genesis 18:20 through 19:29, we see that due to the grievous sins of the people, God had decided to totally destroy the cities of Sodom and Gomorrah. People were going about their daily routines, and they would never have imagined that shortly, just after Lot and his family left Sodom, God would remove these cities from the face of the earth. Lot's uncle, Abraham, bargained with God (Genesis 18:22–32), asking Him to spare the city if He could find as few as ten righteous people. But Lot and his family were the only righteous people to be found. God sent two of His angels to carry out His plans: first, save Lot and his family, then destroy the cities.

Lot met those angels at the gateway of the city and invited them to stay at his house for the night. Before the family and their guests could go to bed, evil men, young and old, surrounded the house and demanded the two visitors be sent out so they could have sex with them. Apparently, homosexuality had become rampant in Sodom. Lot even offered his two virgin daughters in place of the heavenly beings, but the men refused. The angels blinded the men and protected Lot and his family. When the angels asked if he had any other family members, he mentioned his sons-in-law, who were engaged to his daughters. When the young men heard the city was going to be destroyed, they took it as a joke and refused to leave. The angels led Lot, his wife, and their daughters out of the city with a warning—not to look back—but his wife apparently couldn't resist the temptation and looked back and was immediately turned into a pillar of salt (Genesis 19:26). Once Lot had reached a safe place, Sodom and Gomorrah were completely destroyed by burning sulfur (Genesis 19:23–25).

Just as some of Lot's own family members (his sons-in-law) stayed behind due to their lack of faith and unbelief, some of our own family members might do the same today if the situation were to repeat itself. All of this information was written in the Bible for our benefit so that, hopefully, we would be wise enough to read it and learn from it and avoid making the same mistakes as the people who lived during the days of Noah and Lot. Apostle Paul states, "For everything that was written in the past was written to teach us, so that through endurance and the encouragement of the Scriptures we might have hope" (Romans 15:4).

Jesus said there will be wars and rumors of wars, and nations will rise up against nations (Mark 13:7–8; Luke 21:9–10); lately, this has become part of our everyday life. For example, in spite of the fact that Mahatma Gandhi (the "Great Soul," a peacemaker) sacrificed and suffered over thirty years of his life trying to guarantee the peace and freedom of his nation after about three hundred years of British control, the British left the land of India divided into two parts, East and West Pakistan and India; and shortly afterward, West Pakistan separated from the East and became Bangladesh.

The great USSR was also divided into several different nations, and now, for the past couple of years, Africa and the Middle East have been in an uproar, yet the people in those places would never have dreamed that such devastation could happen in their own homeland. *Who knows which country will be the next in line?* Who imagined that the next one would be Syria? What devastation has come to that country from where Apostle Paul started his three missionary journeys!

Lately, a war erupted between Russia and Ukraine. It's been over a year, and it is still going on strong. Thousands and thousands of lives have been lost; cities are flattened. Really, a heartbreaking devastation! I wrote this portion on March 9th, 2023.

The end days present signs, "There will be great earthquakes, famines and pestilences in various places, and fearful events and great signs from heaven" (Luke 21:11). Earthquakes are catastrophic events that cause massive destruction on the earth and death. Today, they are increasing not only in frequency but also in severity. We see three perfect examples of this: the tsunami in Asia and Japan and the quakes in Haiti.

As I wait on the Lord to guide me to the right publishing house, I have been observing the disasters occurring in the world since 2021, and they are as follows: Haiti, the island, was hit with a devastating earthquake for the second time in sixteen years (7.2 on Ritcher scale). Pakistan was hit by a major earthquake, and the latest one was in Turkey and Syria with great devastation; hundreds of buildings collapsed, and thousands of lives were lost. What a heartbreaking situation!

The western region of America (California) has been burning like hell for months as if an unquenchable fire! Many firefighters risked their lives; my heart goes out to them and their families. In 2022, one side of California, where it had never snowed before, was hit by a severe snowstorm, while the other side suffered from floods and mudslides.

Sixteen years later another hurricane hit the southwest and northeast regions of America, flooded, and collapsed many cities and suburban areas.

Record-breaking freezing temperatures and snowstorms in various parts of America, like Texas and Buffalo in New York.

In 2023, Mississippi suffered a huge disaster due to that humongous tornado; only by the grace of God did many survive. The list just goes on and on; I see it as the end days are getting closer and closer, for natural disasters are occurring more frequently with severe devastation.

Revelation, the last book in the Bible, was written by Apostle John. While on the island of Patmos, God showed him in a vision all that was to take place in the future, including the great earthquakes,

> *At that very hour there was a severe earthquake and a tenth of the city collapsed. Seven thousand people were killed in the earthquake, and the survivors were terrified and gave glory to the God of heaven.*
>
> **Revelation 11:13**
> **(Emphasis added by the author)**

Apostle writes again,

> *Then there came flashes of lightning, rumblings, peals of thunder and a severe earthquake. No earthquake like it has ever occurred since man has been on earth, so tremendous was the quake. The great city split into three parts, and the cities of the nations collapsed.*
>
> **Revelation 16:18–19
> (Emphasis added by the author)**

Lately, meteorologists have been reporting about lightning occurring more frequently than ever; also, the hailstones have increased in size of golf balls, some as big as softballs. It is possible that gradually, it could keep increasing its size, for John the apostle wrote what would take place on the day of the Lord, "From the sky huge hailstones of about a hundred pounds each fell upon men" (Revelation 16:21).

Just as Jesus said in Luke 21:11, famines occurring around the globe today are also devastating to the inhabitants of the areas where the earthquakes take place. Many countries are in financial ruin, their populations suffering from severe famine and dying of starvation due to crop failures caused by extreme changes in the weather, such as hurricanes, tornadoes, massive floods, droughts, and unusually cold temperatures.

And today, we see great pestilences occurring like never before, and many are caused by various viruses and bacteria that were thought to have been eradicated. Now, unfortunately, they are resurfacing, and new ones are developing for which there are no known cures. Mad cow disease, AIDS, West Nile virus, flesh-eating diseases, cholera, malaria, smallpox, tuberculosis, leprosy, bubonic plague, and many more of these life-threatening diseases have reached epidemic proportions in many countries. During the process of completing this book, other deadly viruses have surfaced, like Ebola and Zika. As I wait to publish this book, another deadly virus, coronavirus, erupted in one country in 2019 and spread to almost all over the world in 2020. During this pandemic episode, millions of lives were taken in the nick of time, many businesses closed down, reached the unemployment rate at the highest point, causing a financial crash, and lost many people's houses and livelihoods. The saddest of all, many couldn't afford to put the food on the table and had to wait in line for miles and miles for hours to get some free food. Thought to be that New York City would never sleep but ended up in complete lockdown for weeks. Scientists are struggling to find vaccines/medicine for a cure, vaccines to stop the spread, and to prevent reoccurring. I wonder how devastating it would be the next episode of the pandemic!

My beloved, isn't it time to humble yourself, turn to Jesus in a repenting heart, and accept Him as your Lord and Savior? For we don't know when it will be our last breath! Neither our doctor could tell us, nor even a scientist, for the power of life and death is in the hands of the life-giver—our Creator!

Just think, Jesus warned the disciples that because of their relationship with Him, before these things took place, they would experience suffering and persecution, such as flogging, mocking, prejudice, imprisonment, and ultimately even crucifixion (Luke 21:12–13). And it was truly fulfilled in the first century itself; James, brother of John, was beheaded (Act 12:2). If you would kindly read 2 Corinthians 11:23 through the end, the apostle Paul lists the persecution he had endured as a result of preaching the gospel; to name a few, frequently he was imprisoned, exposed to cold and nakedness, he received five times thirty-nine lashes from his own people, the Jews; multiple times he was in shipwrecks, often he was without food and drink, the list just goes on and on. I understood from this why Jesus said, "If anyone would come after me, he must deny himself and take up his cross and follow me" (Matthew 16:24). What a sacrifice! All the apostles except John were martyred.

Jesus also said the gospel would be preached to all the nations before He returns (Matthew 24:14). As we all know, Christian missionaries (like Saint Billy Graham, now in heaven) are continuously risking their lives as they work to spread the Word of God all over the world. Even today, there are billions of people all around the world who have not heard about Jesus, so there is still plenty of work that needs to be done. Jesus is telling us He needs workers in His harvest field right now (Matthew 9:37–38). Are you willing? If you are unable to do the work physically, there are many organizations that need your financial assistance in spreading the gospel. Thanks be to modern technology and those zealous men like Dr. Paul Crouch who jeopardized his house to start the first twenty-four-hour Christian television channel in 1974 in California, USA. And now he has satellites all over the world. What a great soul! (He too has gone to be with the heavenly Father, but now his son continues to do the unfinished work.)

In the Gospels, Jesus repeatedly warned the disciples to watch out, and they asked, "Tell us, when will these things be? And what will be the sign of Your coming, and of the end of the age?" Jesus responded, "Take heed that no one deceives you. For many will come in My name, saying, 'I am the Christ,' and will deceive many" (Matthew 24:3–5, NKJV). (This is recorded in Mark 13:4–6 and Luke 21:7–8; please read.) Jesus continually emphasized that we should always be on guard, "Watch therefore, and pray always that you may be counted worthy to escape all these that will come to pass, and *to stand before the Son of Man*" (Luke 21:36, NKJV) (emphasis added by the author).

No one knows the year, month, day, or hour when the Son of Man will return, except God the Father (Matthew 24:36; Mark 13:32; Acts 1:7). Jesus knows that we are often prone to be preoccupied and unaware of what is happening in the world and yet we

THE GREAT DAY OF THE LORD

need to be in a perpetual state of watchfulness, so He gave us many Scriptures and some in parables, to help us prepare for His coming. Jesus uses one simple example even a child could understand, and that is to learn from the fig tree, "As soon as its twigs get tender and its leaves come out, you know that summer is near. *Even so, when you see all these things, you know that it is near, right at the door*" (Matthew 24:32–33) (emphasis added by the author). (Also written in Mark 13:28; Luke 21:29, please read.)

Today, August 10, 2014, as I was reviewing what I'd written down in the past—and now as I hear the news about what's taking place in the world lately—the Holy Spirit truly compelled me to send this book out urgently, for Jesus' spoken words are being fulfilled day by day. For example, Jesus said in Luke 21:11 that pestilences (fatal epidemic diseases) would occur in various places; verses seventeen through nineteen say that men will hate His followers, but He will reward those who stand firm. Jesus continued,

> *When you see Jerusalem being surrounded by armies, you will know that its desolation is near. Then let those who are in Judea flee to the mountains, let those in the city get out, and let those in the country not enter the city.*
>
> **Luke 21:20–21**
> **(Emphasis added by the author)**

Jesus is warning us to be in a perpetual state of alertness.

In our practical life, especially in America, during the summer months, many parents take their kids to the beaches to have some fun, cool off, and relax. Imagine, at first, as parents, you are preoccupied with fixing the beach chairs, umbrellas, towels (you're already in your swimsuit and sunglasses), and finally applying some suntan lotion, and then it occurs to you that your little ones are not around you. Then, in your frantic search, you notice they are about to step into that high-tide water, and you would try to run, but in loose sand, you can't run very fast! Then your heart starts beating too fast, and you become short of breath. At this point, you would stop and scream at the strangers, "Catch my kids," with your hands pointing toward them, for you don't want your little ones to perish in that ocean. As much as you think you love your precious child, our Father God loves us so much more that it even hurts His heart, and He grieves for us when we turn away from Him and choose to follow the devil's way. The Lord doesn't want any soul to perish, and that is the very reason why He is telling us to "watch out" for His warning signs and prepare ourselves to be with Him in heaven.

My beloved, if you're already a child of God, then look around you; your parents, your spouse, children, siblings, friends, relatives, co-workers, or anyone that you know of who doesn't believe in Jesus Christ—pray for them, witness to them what the Lord has done in your life, and encourage them to receive Jesus as their Savior. Who knows? God might transform their heart so they, too, will spend their eternity in heaven. It is never too late. Always remember the thief on the cross alongside Jesus who made his life-saving request to the Savior at the last moment of his life, "Jesus, remember me when you come into your kingdom" (Luke 23:42). What an assurance our Savior gave him in the following verse, "I tell you the truth, today you will be with me in paradise." Lately, I have been wondering how did he get that wisdom to ask, and my prayer is, "Give me the same wisdom to serve You, my Lord," especially in completing this book.

In America, there is a saying that when the groundhog sees his shadow, there will be six more weeks of winter, and if he doesn't, there will be an early spring. So we've got to be ready with our snow shovels, winter boots, jackets, hats, and gloves or with our lightweight spring attire. Just as we should be prepared for the weather, we should be ready and waiting with anticipation for the Lord's return because it could be just any day now; after all, we are seeing the prophecies being fulfilled more and more frequently now. Whether we live in this world until the Lord returns or leave before His coming, we must prepare ourselves because the living and the dead will meet Jesus in the air at the same time, and we will all be judged according to our faith and our deeds.

Therefore, to stand against the devil's evil schemes, we must always be totally equipped and clothed in the full armor of God, as Saint Paul wrote,

> *Stand firm then, with the belt of truth buckled around your waist, with the breastplate of righteousness in place, and with your feet fitted with the readiness that comes from the gospel of peace. In addition to all this, take up the shield of faith, with which you can extinguish all the flaming arrows of the evil one. Take the helmet of salvation and the sword of the Spirit, which is the word of God.*
>
> **Ephesians 6:14–17**
> **(Emphasis added by the author)**

Oh, what powerful instruction!

When we look at the Old Testament, we can see that many times, the Lord warned the Israelites to get rid of their wickedness and idol worship and return to Him, but the people often remained disobedient, and His wrath rested upon them. Because our loving God is so merciful and compassionate, He could not bear to watch His people suffer. Therefore, whenever they cried out to Him in repentance, He forgave them.

The Lord not only forgave the Israelites, His chosen people, but He also forgave all those who feared Him and repented of their sins. Consider the Ninevites, who were the worst enemies of the Israelites. When God saw the wickedness of the people of Nineveh, He sent His prophet Jonah to that great city to preach against it. When the Ninevites heard that God was going to destroy their city within forty days, they chose to believe the Lord's message. They repented of their sins, declared a fast, and everyone put on sackcloth, from the greatest to the least.

When the king of Nineveh heard the message from God, "He arose from his throne and laid aside his robe, covered himself with sackcloth and sat in ashes" (Jonah 3:6, NKJV). This showed humility. Although the people had already declared a fast, the king ordered that not a man or beast should eat or drink anything, and they would be covered with sackcloth. The king continued,

> *Let everyone call urgently on God. Let them give up their evil ways and their violence. Who knows? God may yet relent and with compassion turn from his fierce anger so that we will not perish.*
>
> **Jonah 3:8b–9**
> **(Emphasis added by the author)**

The king was right. When God saw what the people had done, how they had turned from their wicked ways, He was compassionate and did not bring upon them the destruction He had threatened. What a loving God we have. He wants us all to be obedient to Him and lead a righteous life. Although that may seem difficult at first, when we fear the Lord, nothing is impossible. The longer we practice being obedient, the easier it is, until eventually, it becomes a habit, and ultimately, we find it to be our natural response. God does only what is best for us, so even if we have to be disciplined, we can rest assured that it's for our good.

My friend, try your best to put yourself in God's place. Although He is God Almighty, He is still our loving Father, the One who created us, the One who knows better than anyone else what it takes to make us happy and what we need to survive. Our Father loves us and gives us countless blessings: the air to breathe, food to eat, our families and friends, our homes and our jobs, the freedoms that enable us to work, go to school, or take a vacation, the sun, moon, and stars in the sky, all the planets, the earth with all kinds of minerals in it, the deserts, the forests, the trees, and all the many species of animals, the flowers, the birds in the air, the rain, and the snow, the green pastures, mountains, hills, and valleys, and the lakes, streams, rivers, seas, oceans, and all that is in them. Truly, the list could go on and on. And amazingly, because our God is no respecter of persons, even unbelievers are exposed to these same blessings (Matthew 5:45).

We find in Matthew 24:21–24 that this world will experience distress unequaled since the beginning of the creation. Things would become so unbearable if those days were not cut short, but God, in His mercy, will decrease that period of time for the sake of His children. During the last days, the false Christs and the false prophets will come on the scene. There will be massive confusion among the people due to the great wonders and miraculous signs these deceivers will be performing. Soon, there will be more fearful things happening in the sky. As terrible as that of Noah's time had to have been, it will be even worse, not by flood but by fire; we have never experienced the sun turning black, the moon turning red, the stars falling, nor the rolling up of the sky. Wow! What a dreadful day that will be. Please read the following Bible verses: Isaiah 34:4; Zephaniah 1:14 to the end of the chapter; Mark 13:24–25; Matthew 24:29; Luke 21:25–26; Revelation 6:12–14; and 2 Peter 3:10.

Jesus said,

> *Then people will see the Son of Man coming in clouds with great power and glory. Then he will send his angels all around the earth to gather his chosen people from every part of the earth and from every part of heaven.*
>
> **Mark 13:26–27 (NCV)**
> **(Emphasis added by the author)**

(Also recorded in Luke 21:27.)

Let's see what Jesus, the King of kings, will do when He returns,

> *When the Son of Man comes in his glory, and all the holy angels with Him, then He will sit on the throne of His glory. All the nations will be gathered before Him, and He will separate them one from another, as a shepherd divides his sheep from the goats. And He will set the sheep on His right hand, but the goats on the left. Then the King will say to those on His right hand, 'Come, you blessed of My Father, inherit the kingdom prepared for you from the foundation of the world: for I was hungry and you gave Me food; I was thirsty and you gave Me drink; I was a stranger and you took Me in; I was naked and you clothed Me; I was sick and you visited Me; I was in prison and you came to Me.' "Then the righteous will answer Him, saying, 'Lord, when did we see You hungry and feed You, or thirsty and give You drink? When did we see You a stranger and take You in, or naked and clothe You? Or when did we see You sick, or in prison, and come to You?' And the King will answer and say to them, 'Assuredly, I say to you, inasmuch as you did it to one of the least of these My brethren, you did it to Me.'*
>
> **Matthew 25:31–40 (NKJV)**
> **(Emphasis added by the author)**

Next (continuing with same book and chapter), the Lord will tell the evil ones gathered on His left side, "Depart from Me, you cursed, into the everlasting fire prepared for the devil and his angels" (verse 41, NKJV). Because when the Lord needed help, they ignored His cry. They would immediately protest and say, Lord,

THE GREAT DAY OF THE LORD

when did we see You hungry or thirsty or as a stranger or naked, needing clothes or sick or in prison, and did not help You? (Please read verses 42–44.) The King will reply, "'Assuredly, I say to you, inasmuch as you did not do it to one of the least of these, you did not do it to Me.' *And these will go away into everlasting punishment, but the righteous into eternal life*" (verses 45–46, NKJV) (emphasis added by the author).

This is the moment we are waiting for: where would you like to be? In the hellfire with the devil where there is only weeping and gnashing of teeth (Matthew 24:51), or with Jesus, the King of all kings and Lord of all lords, in His kingdom? Where there is no suffering, no pain, no weeping, nor death (Revelation 21:4). Have you been practicing the above-mentioned good deeds? Although not all, at least a few! For on judgment day, the Lord will reward us according to our deeds. (Please read Revelation 22:12.)

Please do not ignore the poor and the needy; provide them the help they need in any way you can, for the Bible teaches us if we have two shirts, give one to who has none (Luke 3:11). About being in prison, it doesn't have to be a legal prison system. There are people who grieve in their hearts, depressed, lonely, afraid, and isolated, addicted to drugs or alcohol; they all are in their own prison cells. If you know someone with any of these issues, then pray for them and rebuke the devil in the name of the Lord Jesus Christ. You may visit them if possible and have regular telephone conversations. Uplift their spirit with the Word of God and prayers, and provide some material things that could meet their physical needs, showing you truly care for them.

It may be a good idea to meditate daily on the coming of our Lord Jesus and say, "Lord, take me with You when You come." This will help us remember to live a righteous life and grow closer to Him each day so we will not fear, panic, or hide upon His return.

The truth is, I didn't know, until I began to gather data for this book, that the kingdom was prepared for us from the beginning of creation. But I remember having read that Jesus said to His disciples that in His Father's mansion, there are plenty of rooms and that He would go and prepare a place for them (John 14:2). Now I know God created everything at the beginning, but how many millions of years ago? Who knows? What a mighty God! Which human mind can comprehend Him? No wonder Moses said, "A thousand years in your sight are like a day that has just gone by, or like a watch in the night" (Psalm 90:4). One of His attributes is omniscience—He sees things in the past, present, and future at the same time (His understanding is unlimited, infinite), for He is the Alpha and the Omega, the Beginning and the End.

We read in several different places in the book of Revelation, where Jesus Himself said many times that He is coming, including to the six churches (amongst the seven) in Asia Minor. When Jesus saw almost all the churches had already fallen away from His standards, He warned them to repent and return to Him, and Jesus also promised them that they would receive their rewards once they had repented. Every church would receive different rewards if they overcame their falls; as we can see, Jesus said to the church in Ephesus, "To him who overcomes I will give to eat from the tree of life, *which is in the midst of the Paradise of God*" (Revelation 2:7b, NKJV) (emphasis added by the author).

As I was studying this portion, the Holy Spirit brought me back to Adam's situation and helped me realize that when Adam sinned, God took him out of that paradise, for the Lord was concerned that Adam might eat from the tree of life, which was in the middle of the Garden of Eden (Genesis 2:9) and would live forever in his sinful condition. Now I fully understand that God will give the fruit to eat from that very same tree in His appointed time to whom He chooses—those whose hearts are pure and right before Him.

I wonder—if those six churches were not right with God in the first century itself, how about today's churches all over the world? Isn't Jesus telling each and every one of us to get rid of our wickedness, repent, and turn to Him? If we do not willingly turn to Jesus and acknowledge all that He has done to pay for our sins, then His sufferings and death will have all been in vain. The Lord gives us ample time to prepare ourselves, and He is patiently waiting for us to come to Him in repentance, for He does not want any soul to perish (2 Peter 3:9).

I find my knowledge, joy, and strength in the Word of God. That is why I want to encourage everyone else to study the Scriptures. Knowing what God has done in the past always increases our faith in Him. Before you begin to read the Word of God, ask the Holy Spirit to give you an understanding of it, for that is His function. Jesus said, "But the Counselor, the Holy Spirit, whom the Father will send in my name, will teach you all things and will remind you of everything I have said to you" (John 14:26). And again, Jesus said, "But when he, the Spirit of truth, comes, he will guide you into all the truth" (John 16:13a). When we hunger and thirst for the truth, the Holy Spirit will reveal it to us, little by little, for as humans, we are not capable of absorbing it all at once. We are like newborn babies, who must gradually go from their mother's milk to baby food and then on to solid food (1 Peter 2:2). My humble request to you is, my friend, do not remain as a child all your life.

In this world, we have many friends, but as we get to know them better, we tend to surround ourselves with the ones who are honest and sincere. It may take some time (weeks, months, or even years) to find and build a lasting relationship with a trustworthy friend. Likewise, it may take quite a while and great effort to establish the complete trust that it takes to have a loving, personal relationship with God. In order to grow, it is imperative that we constantly study the Scriptures and make them personal and devotional; two thousand years ago, Jesus was speaking to someone else, but today, as you read, He is speaking to you, and you're hearing His voice. That is the feeling you must have. And pray without ceasing. Laziness on our part should never be an excuse for being ignorant of God's Word, for Jesus taught us, "Man does not live on bread alone, but on every word that comes from the mouth of God" (Matthew 4:4).

Is There a Heaven and Hell?

Jesus explained about a very rich man whose name is not mentioned and a poor man, a beggar named Lazarus, in Luke 16:19–31. The wealthy man lived in luxury all his life; he wore very expensive clothes and ate rich, delicious food, whereas Lazarus lay there at this rich man's gate with ulcers all over his body, longing to eat and hoping some food might fall from that rich man's table. After stopping to think about it, I realized that this man was not willingly sharing his food or wealth with the poor and the needy, and he didn't even realize that whatever he had was a gift from God.

Whenever I read, "Even the dogs came and licked his sores" (verse 21b), it always reminds me of Mother Theresa, for if she had been there, she would have placed him on her lap, squeezed out all the pus from every single one of his sores with her bare hands into a bucket, and then she would have dressed them and would have taken him to her shelter to feed him and care for him. What a humble servant of Jesus Christ!

Apparently, the beggar did not suffer too long in this world, and upon his death, the angels took him to Father Abraham's side. (In those days, heaven was called Abraham, Isaac, and Jacob's Bosom; I learned this from the Bible school.) Later, the rich man also died, and he spent his eternity in the fires of hell. He was in torment because there was no one to give him a little water to soothe his burning tongue. When he looked up to heaven, he saw

Lazarus, the beggar, standing with Abraham, and he begged Father Abraham to send Lazarus to help him and his family. Abraham said it was impossible to cross from heaven to hell or vice versa, and there was no point in sending the resurrected Lazarus to his family, for if they didn't listen to Moses, then they wouldn't listen to the beggar, either.

This lesson teaches us that heaven and hell are definitely real, and we will inherit one or the other according to our faith and deeds. Jesus stated emphatically,

> *Behold, I am coming soon! My reward is with me, and I will give to everyone according to what he has done. I am the Alpha and the Omega, the First and the Last, the Beginning and the End.*
>
> **Revelation 22:12–13**
> **(Emphasis added by the author)**

Amen and amen. Come Jesus, come. I'm ready.

CHAPTER 12:

FROM THE BEGINNING TO THE END?

There will never be another prophet like John the Baptist, who came to warn the world, "Repent, for the kingdom of heaven is at hand!" (Matthew 3:2, NKJV). Nor will Jesus Himself ever come back to earth as a teacher. However, there are currently and will continue to be false prophets and false Christs (Matthew 24:11, 24) who, under the power of Satan, try to deceive many people, even the faithful ones. They will perform great wonders and miracles, and their messages will sound totally convincing, but God will punish them on judgment day. Evidence is found; Jesus said,

> *Many will say to Me in that day, 'Lord, Lord, have we not prophesied in Your name, cast out demons in Your name, and done many wonders in Your name?' And then I will declare to them, 'I never knew you; depart from Me, you who practice lawlessness!'*
>
> **Matthew 7:22–23 (NKJV)**
> **(Emphasis added by the author)**

Do not be deceived by those evildoers; instead, have complete faith and courage to stand firm in the *truth of the Word of God*.

All believers must keep in mind, on the last days, if anyone tells you, Jesus Christ is at your neighbor's house, or He is in your driveway, "Do not go out" to look for Him. Or He is in your own guest's room, "Do not believe it" (Matthew 24:26). Those are Jesus' commands; be obedient to Him (don't forget what had happened to Lot's wife when she disobeyed God's command, "Do not look behind" (Genesis 19:17, 26). We must always remember that when Christ, the true Son of God, comes back, He will not set foot upon the earth; instead, He will appear in the clouds with great glory, and He will send His angels all over the world to bring His children up to meet Him in the air (Matthew 24:30–31).

Two thousand years ago, Jesus questioned us, "What good will it be for a man if he gains the whole world, yet forfeits his soul? Or what can a man give in exchange for his soul?" (Matthew 16:26). What a question! Who can answer? And remember the words God spoke through Moses, "If anyone does not listen to my words that the prophet speaks in my name, I myself will call him to account" (Deuteronomy 18:19). Jesus came to teach what the Father wanted the world to know and save the souls, not to judge, for Father will be the judge (John 12:47–50). We will be held accountable if we don't obey Jesus' teachings, and surely, *there will be great consequences.*

Although this book contains a portion of the teachings of Jesus Christ, I encourage you to study the first four books found in the New Testament—Matthew, Mark, Luke, and John—in their entirety so you will gain a more thorough understanding of His message and easier to apply to your daily life.

If you have already studied all four Gospels, then I am sure you understand that Jesus is coming back soon, and it will be at an hour when He is least expected, so be on alert. A perfect example of this unexpected arrival is found in Matthew 25:1–13, the parable of the ten virgins who took their lamps and went out to meet the bridegroom. Of the ten, five were found to be wise, as they came not only with their lamps filled with oil but carried extra oil with them as well because they were not sure of the exact hour that the bridegroom was coming. The other five were fools, for they took the lamps but not sufficient oil.

The bridegroom tarried, and the virgins became weary and fell asleep. At midnight, there came a shout, saying, "Here's the bridegroom! Come out to meet him!" (verse 6). Suddenly, the virgins woke up and lit their lamps; unfortunately, due to lack of oil, the lamps of the foolish ones had been fading away; while they searched for a place to buy oil, the groom arrived. Those who were prepared went inside to celebrate the wedding banquet with the bridegroom. Later, when the unprepared virgins returned, they found the doors had already been locked, and they said, "Sir! Sir! Open the door for us!" (verse 11). Jesus told them, "'I tell you the truth, I don't know you.' Therefore *keep watch*, because you do not know the day or the hour" (verses 12–13) (emphasis added by the author). (Please read Matthew 25:1–13 for better understanding.)

Although this passage does not interpret the meaning of the oil, some biblical scholars...

> See it as representing the Holy Spirit and His work in salvation. Salvation is more than mere profession for it involves regeneration by the Holy Spirit. Those who will merely profess to be saved, and do not actually possess the Spirit, will be excluded from the feast, that is the Kingdom.[1]

Years after I wrote the above, to be exact, on December 2, 2016 morning, I asked the Lord for my daily word, and I opened the Bible. It was Zachariah, chapter four. As I studied intensely, I came to verse six; I greatly rejoiced and praised the Lord Almighty, for He revealed to me oil represents God's Spirit. I quote,

---

[1] John F. Walvoord and Roy B. Zuck, eds., The Bible Knowledge Commentary (Colorado Springs: Cook Communication Ministries, 2004), 80.

Then he (the angel) said to me, This [addition of the bowl to the candlestick, causing it to yield a ceaseless supply of oil from the olive trees] is the word of the Lord to Zerubbabel, saying, Not by might, nor by power, but by My Spirit [of Whom the oil is a symbol], says the Lord of hosts.

Zachariah 4:6 (AMP)
(Emphasis added by the author)

(Please read from the beginning of Zachariah chapter 4 for a better understanding.)

Jesus has taught us many similar parables regarding those who will be eligible to enter His kingdom and those who will receive everlasting punishment. Many other teachings on this subject can be found in the following Gospels (please read Matthew 24:40–51, 25:14–30; Luke 12:35–48).

Although I knew a little bit about the Word of God at the time I began to write this book, it became my constant prayer both at home and before going to my writer, "Lord, unless You give me the message, I cannot write Your book." Then I would open the Bible, as if He was directing my fingers, for each time, He would take me to different books with new and exciting messages that would strengthen me and carry me through each day's circumstances (writings) (subjects). What a faithful and awesome God! I still continue to pray earnestly, "Lord, give me Your wisdom, knowledge, and understanding, and fill my writer and me with Your Holy Spirit." When Carolyn and I got together, even before we started writing, we would always pray. Sometimes, when I had difficulty telling her what to write, we would pray again. This has been Carolyn's continuous prayer for me, "Father, please put Your thoughts in Leela's head, Your words in her mouth, and Your meditations in her heart." My dear readers, the Lord gave me everything He wanted me to write in His book from start to finish, and that is why I must tell you, the author of this book is *my God and my King*—I'm just a messenger. Carolyn calls herself a "fifty-nine-cent Bic pen." I want to give the Lord all the praise, honor, and glory for using me as His instrument to write His book. There are truly not enough words to thank Him for this huge privilege and awesome blessing.

I consider myself to be poor in reading, writing, communicating, vocabulary, and poor in computer skills, but I know I am a mourning woman, for I brokenheartedly cry out to the Lord, always seeking God in my everyday life in every way I can. There are many times I have failed, for I am nowhere close to perfection. Whenever I use my own filthy will, I hurt others with my words or deeds. He never fails to lift me up by sending His Holy Spirit to convict me of my sins. I have always immediately and shamelessly asked forgiveness from those whom I've hurt. I thank God for revealing these things to me. For many years, I have asked the Lord to remind me of my sins; at times, He has even taken me back to my younger age to remind me of something I had forgotten. At the remembrance of those things, I would repent and often be in tears.

When I studied the book of Ezekiel, the Holy Spirit gave me the understanding of how vitally important it is to confess our sins and live a righteous life,

> *But if a wicked man turns away from all the sins he has committed and keeps all my decrees and does what is just and right, he will surely live; he will not die. None of the offenses he has committed will be remembered against him. Because of the righteous things he has done, he will live. Do I take any pleasure in the death of the wicked? declares the Sovereign LORD. Rather, am I not pleased when they turn from their ways and live? But if a righteous man turns from his righteousness and commits sin and does the*

same detestable things the wicked man does, will he live? None of the righteous things he has done will be remembered. Because of the unfaithfulness he is guilty of and because of the sins he has committed, he will die.

Ezekiel 18:21–24
(Emphasis added by the author)

I love everything except the last verses, which truly scare me, for I feel at times, we Christians consider ourselves as righteous, as the Pharisees in Jesus' time, and there are times when we turn away from our faith to do evil things and gain fame, wealth, or worldly pleasure. Some have even gone so far; they have brought about massive destruction and death. Perfect examples of this madness were David Koresh and Jim Jones, who led huge crowds of people to their deaths. Under the power of Satan and his evil, these men convinced their own followers to take their lives, supposedly all in the name of God.

Lately, my prayer and struggle have been to remove filthy character traits from me, such as pride, jealousy, impatience, rash reactions, anger, and anything else that is not right with God. I want God to replace those traits with humbleness, love, joy, peace, patience, increased faith, self-control, and honesty, for I don't want to sin. I have been trying to eliminate one sin at a time so that I may not repeat the sins of the past. When the thought comes to my mind to do something that is not right before God, by the power of the Holy Spirit, I say, "Devil, I rebuke you in the name of the Lord Jesus Christ—get out from me." It truly works, but the same sinful thoughts will haunt me weeks, months, or even years later. Of course, I have failed a few times, but I ask God prayerfully and brokenheartedly for forgiveness. I also ask forgiveness from the person I sinned against. By the power of the Holy Spirit, I have been sinning less and less; oh, what a peace it is! You, too, may want to try and see how effective it will be. It could be anything from telling lies to sexual immorality, addiction to alcohol, drugs, gambling, or even food. Meditate and practice this word of God to strengthen you, "A wise man fears the LORD and shuns evil" (Proverbs 14:16a). If we truly fear the Lord, the Holy Spirit will empower us and control us from sinning.

Writing this book, I have gained a wealth of knowledge because the Father has kept feeding me with spiritual truth. Even my writer has obtained more wisdom and understanding (although she already had a vast supply of knowledge, for she studied under many wonderful Bible teachers who graduated from Dallas Theological Seminary). You may think that my journey with Carolyn has been an easy one, but on the contrary, at times, we had arguments over the wording or sometimes even the context. Then, we would usually take a break, eat, and return to work prayerfully. I can remember a few times that we actually took a hiatus for several days. In the meantime, I would be praying for Carolyn, "Lord, give her Your wisdom, knowledge, and understanding. Please help her to write exactly the way You want it to be written." He faithfully answered my prayers.

A Faithful God

When I was young, I served my parents. When I reached middle age, I served my husband and children. Although I was an active member of my church during all those years, as I approached the age of retirement, I had an overwhelming desire to serve the Lord completely for the rest of my life. It soon became my utmost priority. Now, I am totally and completely surrendered to serving Him. My prayer has always been, "Father, here I am, make use of me." To this day, I still remember, as I prepared to move to Georgia, the Sunday school headmistress in New York who gave me a send-off speech, "Leela has chosen the best, like Mary" (for better understanding, please read Luke 10:38–42). She knew I chose to go to the Bible school to satisfy my hunger and thirst for the Word of God.

When I look back, I am truly amazed, for it was all by God's wonderful grace. I now see that my own personal experiences have brought me to a much deeper understanding of Jeremiah,

> *The word of the LORD came to me, saying, "Before I formed you in the womb I knew you, before you were born I set you apart; I appointed you as a prophet to the nations." "Ah, sovereign LORD," I said, "I do not know how to speak; I am only a child."*
>
> **Jeremiah 1:4–6**
> **(Emphasis added by the author)**

I was totally astonished to find that the prophet and I had almost the exact response to the Lord's calling. I felt from the start of this book that this assignment should have been given to a biblical scholar, not me—and yet, with all my weaknesses, the Lord still chose and used me to accomplish His purpose and His plan. So, my beloved readers, my prayer to the Lord for you is that you study the Word of God, seek Jesus Christ constantly and wholeheartedly, stay in prayer, and know that the Lord will always be with you. And may your heart be attentive to His calling.

Now, let me share with you some of the awesome answers to prayer that I've had. In one of the earlier chapters of this book, I wrote about the struggles my husband and I were having regarding going to church. After we married, Simon started right off by missing our first Easter and Christmas service and many Sunday worship meetings. I didn't have the same relationship with the Lord that I have today. Not only did I not know how to pray for my husband, but I didn't even know I had to pray for him; instead, I concentrated on myself. I felt like God should feel empathy toward me; after all, He knew what I was going through.

FROM THE BEGINNING TO THE END?

In 2003, I saw a book titled *Praying God's Will for My Husband* by Lee Roberts; I was extremely excited and purchased it right away. I immediately began to search through it and to underline the areas where I felt Simon needed my prayers the most. From that time on, I began fervently praying for Simon. Although there were some gradual changes in his behavior in response to those prayers, a complete transformation took place by 2008. Since then, it has come to the point where he doesn't want to miss church. Simon has been totally transformed, evidenced by the miraculous peace that has flooded our home. Even that once-dreaded trip to church has now become enjoyable due to supernatural peace.

My husband is truly blessed, for he was born with a beautiful singing voice. At times, he sang for two or three people; on other occasions, he might sing for a very large crowd. Regardless of the size of the audience, he always sang from his heart. He truly enjoyed singing the songs made popular by Mohammed Rafi, and eventually, he became known as Mohammed Rafi of Kerala. His voice is a gift from God; I have been praying and encouraging him to use his voice to glorify the Lord. Now, by the grace of God, during our evening devotions, he takes the hymnal and begins to sing with no prompting from me. A treasured moment for me was when Simon instructed me on how to improve the way I was singing one of my favorite songs. When he helped me change the tune and the rhythm, the song brought me greater joy.

Once my son, Simon Jr., reached the higher end of the age bracket for marriage, my constant prayer for him and his sister became, "Do not cut off our generation, Lord, but multiply them." For Psalmist said, "He will bless those who fear the LORD—small and great alike. May the LORD make you increase, both you and your children" (Psalm 115:13–14). And again, we read, "May you live to see your children's children" (Psalm 128:6). I prayed, asking the Father, "Please, show us a godly woman for him and a godly man for her; give them an average life, neither rich nor poor;

above all, do not let them turn away from You."

In August 2009, Maureen came home on vacation, and as usual, we had our family devotions each morning and evening. She had only been home for a couple of days when she told me that, apparently, I wasn't praying the right prayers because nothing had been happening with respect to her finding a husband.

The next day, Maureen, her dad, and I went to Barnes & Noble. While they were looking around, I went to the Christian section and found a book called *The Power of Praying for Your Adult Children* by Stormie Omartian. I was surprised that the store had just the right book for me at just the right time. It was almost as if God Himself had put it on the shelf.

After showing the book to Maureen and seeing her enthusiastic reaction, I made the purchase. Although the contents of the book were very similar to my own prayers, the author used more of God's Word in her prayers, and her English was much better than mine. That same night, we began using some of the prayers from our newly purchased book. Before Maureen left, she mentioned how much she missed our family prayer time. She suggested we continue with it once she got back to New York. It was such a great joy to hear those thoughts from my daughter, and we quickly resumed our family prayers over the telephone.

Now, I pray for the following:

My Jewish friends all over the world, God will open their spiritual eyes to the truth of His Word, and they will realize their long-awaited Messiah came over two thousand years ago. I pray that they will not be as God spoke of them to Isaiah, "Be ever hearing, but never understanding; be ever seeing, but never perceiving" (Isaiah 6:9). And I read these passages spoken by Jesus,

> *O Jerusalem, Jerusalem, you who kill the prophets*
> *and stone those sent to you, how often I have longed*

> *to gather your children together, as a hen gathers her chicks under her wings but you were not willing. Look, your house is left to you desolate. For I tell you, you will not see me again until you say, 'Blessed is he who comes in the name of the Lord.'*
>
> **Matthew 23:37–39**
> **(Emphasis added by the author)**

(Luke also has recorded this in his book, 13:34–35.)

I'm always reminded of just how much the Lord loves the Jewish people, and I cry out, "Father, please, open their hearts and help them obey Your instructions."

How would you feel if your son refused to obey you and ran away, but years later, he returned, crying out to you with repentance? Wouldn't you accept him wholeheartedly and celebrate because once he was lost, and now he's found? That is exactly the kind of parent our God is. If you take one step toward Jesus, then He will take a thousand steps to come to you and hold you in His arms—He will never let you go. He is a loving and compassionate God, and He longs for you. A perfect example of the Father's love is depicted in Luke 15:11 to the end of the chapter (please read).

My Muslim friends, you are so blessed, for you are the offspring of Father Abraham. You and the entire world have been truly blessed by the promise the Lord made to Abram. Through his seed, all nations will be saved. By this very same covenant, my ancestors and I have also been blessed to receive Jesus (the Seed) as our Savior and turn away from idol worship; thus, we, the Gentiles, also became the children of Father Abraham. Jesus, who was both Man and God, in His humility, took all the punishment we deserved, carried our sins to the cross, and died in our place. On the third day, He was raised from the dead, went back to heaven, and is seated at the right side of the Father. Jesus Christ, the Creator of all, was the God of Abraham, who, at the age of ninety-nine, chose to believe the Lord when God told him that he and Sarah would have a son within a year (please read Genesis 18:1–15). Dear friends, I pray to the Lord you will be as faithful and obedient to God as Father Abraham was. I pray you will trust in Jesus Christ, not as a prophet, but as your personal Savior and Lord. May He give you the peace that surpasses all understanding, and may He shelter you under the shadow of His wings. In Jesus' name, I pray, amen.

If you would kindly read the book of Hebrews, which was written sometime between AD 60 and 70, you will have a better understanding of who Jesus Christ was, is, and will be forever. As a foretaste of what you will be reading, I quote,

> *In the past God spoke to our forefathers through the prophets at many times and in various ways, but in these last days he has spoken to us by his Son, whom he appointed heir of all things, and through whom he made the universe. The Son is the radiance of God's glory and the exact representation of his being, sustaining all things by his powerful word.*
>
> **Hebrews 1:1–3c**
> **(Emphasis added by the author)**

As we continue reading, verse four states that He was much superior to the angels. We again read in Hebrews, "So Christ was sacrificed once to take away the sins of many people; and he will appear a second time, not to bear sin, but to bring salvation to those who are waiting for him" (Hebrews 9:28). I hope and pray that you, my friends, will be among them.

My Hindu friends, I'm not writing this to convert you, for that is far beyond my ability. Only God can change the heart of man. However, my request to you is to read the Holy Bible and read it for your own pleasure. I suggest from my experience that you start with the book of Luke and then read the book of Acts, the third and the fifth books in the New Testament; they were both written by the same man—Luke—inspired by the Spirit of God. He was highly educated in those days—a physician (Colossians 4:14); he interviewed many who were eyewitnesses to Jesus' birth, His missionary works, death, resurrection, and ascension to heaven, and he wrote them in detail and in chronological order. Before Luke came to know Jesus Christ, he was a Grecian Gentile, a pagan/idol worshipper just like us.

The Holy Bible says that idols are manmade,

> *They have mouths, but cannot speak, eyes, but they cannot see; they have ears but they cannot hear, noses, but they cannot smell, they have hands, but cannot feel, feet, but they cannot walk; nor can they utter a sound with their throats.*
>
> **Psalm 115:5–7**
> **(Emphasis added by the author)**

Isn't it true? I pray that God will change the hearts of many as He did with Luke and my ancestors. Jesus died on the cross for our sins and rose from the dead on the third day. He is the Creator of all, including you. He is the living God.

My dear Buddhist friends, although, at a young age, I studied in school about Siddhartha, also known as Sri Buddha, I can't remember much of it. But I thank God for modern technology and Google. It gave me a better understanding of his life, his ideology, his teachings, and his practical life. He was born in the northern part of India, and he was brought up as a Hindu. By the time Buddha was of twenty-nine years old, God showed him the purpose of his life on this earth and gave him a humble heart. Instead of becoming a king, he lowered himself to be a servant of God. He never claimed to be God, but he taught and guided the people to spiritual awakening. He taught there was no intermediary between humans and the divine; one must strive for it with the knowledge and understanding of reality. What an awesome message!

Now let me introduce you to a greater teacher than Sri Buddha or anyone in the world—He is not of this world but God Himself, the divine power, the Creator of all (including Sri Buddha). He humbled Himself and came down from heaven to save us from our sins and give us eternal life. His name is Jesus Christ. As Sri Buddha said, there is no intermediary between man and God; we are tremendously blessed to have a direct relationship with the Lord Jesus Christ. He not only taught and preached how to attain salvation for our spirit; He healed every kind of sickness and performed many wonders and miracles. Jesus demonstrated through His life how to overcome calamities and how to be victorious over evildoers. He didn't stop there; He showed His love for all mankind by giving His life, shedding His blood, carrying our sins on the cross, and dying for our salvation. But He rose from the dead and lives forever and ever.

I request that you, my friends, study Jesus' teachings from the Holy Bible, the books of Matthew, Mark, Luke, and John. So, with knowledge and understanding, you, too, can attain salvation.

To all the readers of this book: King Solomon, the wisest man on Earth, wrote from his life experience, most likely in 935 BC, "'Meaningless! meaningless!' says the Teacher. 'Utterly meaningless! Everything is meaningless'" (Ecclesiastes 1:2). He continued,

> *Now all has been heard; here is the conclusion of the matter: Fear God and keep his commandments, for this is the whole duty of man. For God will bring every deed into judgment, including every hidden thing, whether it is good or evil.*
>
> **Ecclesiastes 12:13–14**
> **(Emphasis added by the author)**

We see its comparison in the New Testament, "Nothing in all

creation is hidden from God's sight. Everything is uncovered and laid bare before the eyes of him to whom we must give account" (Hebrews 4:13). How true it is! Let us listen to our Master's voice.

> *But I tell you that men will have to give account on the day of judgment for every careless word they have spoken. For by your words you will be acquitted, and by your words you will be condemned.*
>
> **Matthew 12:36–37**
> **(Emphasis added by the author)**

(Please read from verses 33 onward for better understanding)

So, we ought to be extremely cautious in our conduct.

Dear friends, you may be sitting in front of a computer with closed doors, working on your favorite website, such as pornography, or maybe stealing somebody's identity, and still others plotting destruction, whatsoever it may be, thinking no one is watching you. Do not be fooled. God is omnipresent, omniscient and omnipotent. You can't hide from Him. He is present everywhere and sees every letter you click on with each finger on the keyboard. He knows the motives of your heart before you've even completed a word (please read Psalm 139:1–14; in fact, read its entirety; it's so good). So, be aware, on judgment day, we all will face the Righteous Judge, Jesus, the King of kings, who will give us our reward—either eternal life or eternal punishment—according to our deeds. Please, as your friend, sister, mother, or grandmother, I humbly request you to get rid of your ungodliness, wickedness, and violence, and in repentance, ask God the Father for forgiveness. Then, invite Jesus Christ into your heart as the Lord and Savior, for my heart desires that you spend your eternity with your Creator in heaven.

Lastly, I pray that the whole world, including atheists and those who have never accepted Jesus Christ, would invite Him into their hearts as their Lord and Savior. Do not stop there, but continue to study the Word of God, for with knowledge and understanding, you will increase your faith, spiritual strength, and courage to stand firm in the Word of Truth. Talk to Him constantly, have a deep personal relationship with Him, and be blessed! Hallelujah.

When I started writing this chapter, I thought this would be the conclusion of this book. But God had other plans, so please keep reading.

CHAPTER 13:

GOD'S AMAZING MERCY

I was just about to complete chapter 12 when I started having some health problems, and because my physical condition began to deteriorate so rapidly, it became necessary to plan a trip to India, where I could receive Ayurvedic (naturopathic) treatments. I booked my plane ticket with a departure date of May 23, 2012, and a return date of August 8, 2012.

As soon as I told Carolyn I was going, she began praying that the Lord would use me mightily on the entire trip, even while waiting in the airport; she prayed He would seat me next to someone on the plane whom I could encourage or lead to Jesus. Little did I know, when I left, the amazing plans He had in store for me and my family.

My younger sister, Valsamma, met me at the airport, and I was looking forward to staying in her home, not only because we would be going for Ayurvedic treatments together but because we would have the opportunity to continue the family tradition of every morning and evening prayers, singing hymns, and reading the Scriptures. During these times of prayer, I never failed to ask God to use my sister and me in serving Him anytime and anywhere.

During one of our conversations, my sister mentioned that she had given one of her tenants, Shyba, a Bible before she left for

America. Valsamma told Shyba to read it while she was gone, and when she returned, Valsamma would try to answer any questions she might have. It is very important to note that this young woman had been Hindu eight years before; she converted to Christianity in order to marry her boyfriend, who was a Catholic.

After Valsamma introduced us, Shyba informed me that she had never opened that Bible, for she had no idea of what to look for or where to begin; she also told me that she would love to learn the Bible, but she had no one to teach her. The moment I heard this, I realized what she was going through, for I had been in a similar situation before I went to Bible school. I was overjoyed at the thought of teaching her. I immediately said, "Starting tomorrow, I'll teach you every day for an hour." She was extremely happy and excitedly accepted. I told her to come prepared with her Bible, along with paper and pen, to take notes (little did I know the volume of notes she would be taking).

That same night, in the quietness of my room, I cried out to the Lord and said, "Father, You know that she knows nothing. Where do I begin, and what shall I teach her? Please, give me Your wisdom, guidance, and direction that I, in turn, may teach her all You want her to know." While I was still praying, the Lord spoke to my heart and said, "Begin to teach *why Jesus came to this world.*" That led me to the book of Genesis, the creation, the fall of Adam and Eve, and the first promise regarding Jesus' coming that God the Father ever made: the Lord said to the serpent (the devil), "And I'll put enmity between you and the woman, and between your offspring and hers; he will crush your head, and you will strike his heel" (Genesis 3:15). The following day when she came, I was completely prepared with notes and Bible references. Before we began our study time, we held hands and prayed together. As the days went by, her hunger and thirst for the Word of God became stronger and stronger. What started out as a one-hour study time became one and a half hours, then two, and, before we knew it, three.

One day, while I was praying, the Lord put it in my heart to teach her the book of Ruth. I thought that it was so ironic, for in her book, chapter one, verse sixteen, Ruth, a Gentile, tells her Jewish mother-in-law, Naomi, "Your people will be my people and your God my God." In like manner, Shyba made her own personal sacrifices by leaving her idol worship, accepting her husband's living God, and merging with his family. I explained to her, "God gave me this very special message just for you." She was very humbled and yet joyful. What an awesome student—she not only did the homework I assigned, but she always did much more. She was also very adept at memorization and loved to be quizzed, which highly motivated her. Today, after I returned to America, when I talk to her by phone, she still studies the Scriptures daily and understands it more and more. She misses me and can't wait for me to come next year so that I can teach her even more.

August was approaching; I was perked up after the Ayurvedic treatment. I was determined to leave India on the eighth so I could attend a women's conference in Orlando, Florida. I am the leader of the women's league at my church and have the responsibility of taking groups of women to conferences. As I was preparing to return home, my sister informed me that she felt very strongly that I should stay. She compelled me to take care of my family matters now. She said, "Do not worry about the church business, for there are others who can handle it. While you are still here, call your children and tell them to come over; otherwise, they will never get married." She knew that both Maureen and Simon had been searching for spouses on various marriage websites for over five years. My sister loved both my children very much; in fact, she always told people how they were sweet, loving, honest, kind, and of great moral character.

For several years, we had all been making every effort to find suitable spouses for Maureen and Simon. We even ran an ad in the Indian newspaper in October 2010. In response to that ad, I received many telephone calls and e-mails. One of them was from a widow in India whose son and daughter lived in London. Ultimately, Simon began communicating with her daughter, and after a few months, the mother suggested that Simon could marry her daughter, and her son could marry Maureen. I informed the mother that unless they could actually see each other physically, a marriage could never take place. As a result of our conversation, she sent both her son and daughter to America in July 2011, but to no avail—after two or three days of sightseeing and interacting, both Simon and Maureen sadly realized that these people were not their life partners.

One day, my sister told me that after her daughter's marriage, the Lord burdened her heart to start praying for Maureen. For over ten years, she had been faithfully asking the Lord to show us the man He had prepared for her. My two older sisters had also been praying for my children for the last few years. Besides them, my prayer-line sisters had been earnestly praying on a daily basis for my children, as well as my community Bible class group. Now, I had no choice; I obeyed my little sister's wisdom and sent an e-mail to the church, telling them I was extending my vacation due to some family matters. I asked them to pray that God would be merciful to us, as well as asked them to encourage the ladies to attend the conference.

I contacted my husband and children and told them that they needed to prepare to come to India very soon, for I wouldn't be going home again until they made the trip. I explained to Maureen and Simon their number one priority should be finding spouses. After all, most of their friends were already married and had children. I told them that I, as well as Aunt Valsamma and Uncle Philip, would be making every effort to find them both a godly Christian mate. As soon as we found suitable candidates, we would let them know so that they could have conversations with them via the internet, telephone, or Skype. Once they decided on the people they felt were right for them, we would arrange the marriage date, and all must come immediately, for they would not want to risk losing the opportunity. However, I told them they needn't be afraid; marriages would take place only if they felt it was true love after they had met the people face to face. After spending much time in prayer and having some lengthy debates and discussions, Maureen and Simon both agreed to the plan.

The three of us in India began an intense search for young men and women. After a couple of weeks, Valsamma and I talked with the parents of a young lady who called in response to the newspaper ad that we placed for Simon. By the end of the conversation, it sounded like their daughter was a good candidate. We set an appointment to meet with her and her parents at the very famous St. Gregorios Orthodox Church, Parumala. There, the mother reported to us they were regular churchgoers, she led the women's league in their respective church, and her daughter had read through the whole Bible. The young lady was fairly good-looking, educated, well-mannered, and had a pleasing personality. We thought this was the one for Simon. We returned home happily, thanking God. I informed Simon all about the girl and gave him her e-mail address and telephone number for him to contact her. Days later, they started to converse, saw each other's photos on Facebook, and seemed to like one another. The parents were in constant contact with my sister and me, and it seemed like we had fallen in favor with them—we, too, had a good impression of them.

By the middle of August, Simon and his prospective wife had become more serious, and the parents on both sides agreed to make wedding arrangements. We planned the wedding for September 10, 2012, at 11:30 a.m. Ultimately, we found that many weddings were planned for that same day in the Christian community, and it was quite difficult to find a church with a seating capacity of four to five hundred people.

I advised Simon Jr. and Maureen to put in a vacation request and book their tickets as soon as possible. At that point, we had not found a suitable candidate for Maureen, but she was extremely excited about going to her only brother's wedding and helped Simon select his suits, shirts, ties, and shoes.

Simon wasted no time in giving the good news to his direct boss, who was very happy and not only congratulated him but also granted him three weeks of vacation. Next, he contacted the travel agency and booked an airplane ticket to arrive in India on August 27 and return on September 14. Maureen and Simon Sr. also booked tickets to arrive on September 4 and return on September 20. I had already changed my return ticket to September 22.

After everyone had made their reservations and we'd booked the church and the reception hall, unpleasant things started popping up. First, a few days later, Simon became very upset when his second boss said, "Permission denied, and turn in your resignation!"

It was very shocking. I tried to comfort and reassure him by saying, "Simon, God has been so good to you; He is our provider. The Lord will give you an even better job. Don't be concerned; just trust Him."

Slowly, Simon's anxiety began to taper off. Secondly, his future in-laws imposed three demands on us.

I called Simon Sr. and told him what the father had said. I advised him to consider not calling him, for in no way were we going to give in to his rules and regulations. My husband was understandably puzzled by this turn of events. He was concerned because we had already spent thousands of dollars on plane tickets for the sole purpose of attending Simon's wedding. He had told many of the church members, including the priest and our friends.

I told him, "Don't worry. On Sunday, August 27, we will place another ad for Simon and Maureen. We will find new candidates." In any case, Simon had to come to see the proposed girl. If he were pleased, then we could proceed with the marriage; of course, we prayed that God's will would be done. After our discussion, he calmed down. I remembered one day hearing him say he wished the children would marry before he died. I knew he had been praying for hours, morning and evening, for this to take place.

I also informed Father John Thomas, the vicar at Maureen and Simon's parish church, which was our—the parent's—previous parish in New York, of the situation. He had been kept up to date on everything since the beginning. He not only provided marriage counseling for Simon but also advised him not to rush, for there were many girls who were waiting to marry. Father Thomas also gave me the name of his uncle, Father Abraham Tharakan, in India, so that I may contact him in case of emergency or help. I contacted Father Tharakan and told him the details of the situation. His advice was it would be better to avoid this marriage proposal for long-term peace.

Valsamma, Philip, and I were devastated, and yet we all agreed—"We do not want to deal with these people"—despite the fact that we did not find any other suitable prospects for Simon. I felt like they were of this world, not of God, for there was no love or peace in them. Which made me feel very uncomfortable, so I began to pray, "Father, don't let this marriage take place." Suddenly, the Holy Spirit led me to the Lord's Prayer, "Lead us not into temptation, but deliver us from the evil one" (Matthew 6:13). I went to St. George Orthodox Church at Puthuppally. There, I knelt down with my face to the ground and brokenheartedly cried out to the Lord. I also requested the patron of the church, St. George, to pray that this marriage would not take place and "lead us not into temptation, but to deliver us from the evil one." My sister prayed earnestly to the Lord for the family, saying, "They (the family) are coming soon with no certainty of a wedding, but, Lord, may they leave with joyful hearts when they return to America."

Simon had not been to India since he was a little boy when I took him to see his grandparents and all of our other relatives and friends. At last, after twenty-six years, here came Simon to India on Sunday, August 27, at 3:30 a.m. Valsamma and I went to pick him up at the airport. On the way back, I suggested that since it was Sunday, we take the time to stop and pray at St. Mary's Cathedral at Manarcad on the way home. I recommended that we kneel down and pray for the Lord to give him a godly Christian woman as his wife. Simon and I knelt down and bowed in prayer. It was about 7:30 a.m. when we finished praying, and we arrived home in less than ten minutes.

Philip warmly welcomed Simon. They chatted for a short while. Philip then went to visit George, a friend. He wanted to discuss Simon's situation. George told Philip that he had seen a mother and daughter coming from their parish church after attending the first-morning service; it happened to be the exact church where we had prayed earlier that same day. George also stated that the young woman looked quite good, but he was unsure of her age and level of education. He said, "All the neighbors know her as a person of character and good reputation. My advice to you is, go to her home and talk to her parents."

Since it was Sunday, Philip waited until noon for everyone to come home from church after the second service. He then went and talked with both the mother and the father, asking about their daughter's age and educational background. Philip could tell by their answers that their daughter was a suitable candidate for Simon. The mother asked him if this was a marriage proposal, and he replied, "Yes, it's for my wife's nephew, who arrived from America this morning and is presently at my home." Both parents liked the proposal that Philip made. They came to see Simon that same evening, and after the conversation, they invited us to come to their home at 10:30 the next morning to meet their daughter, Teena. Most Indian parents are concerned about the character and morals of the people born and raised in America, but because my sister spoke highly about Simon, she (the mother) accepted and trusted her word.

The following morning, Simon had a long, private conversation with the young lady. When they came out of the meeting, the look on their faces was sheer delight.

The next thing on our agenda was to keep the previously set appointment with the first girl and her parents, which was over an hour's drive. Although I personally wasn't looking forward to this trip, I went to it out of respect for my son—I wanted him to have the chance to compare the two young ladies so that he wouldn't have any regrets later on. After we reached our destination, Simon had the same opportunity to have a private conversation with the first candidate; he told her he would let his mother know his final decision.

On our way home, my husband's nephew, Jacob, asked Simon who he felt was the best candidate for him and why. Simon told him it was the first person he had seen that morning because she was very honest, humble, and lovable. My heart was overjoyed that my son had made a decision, and at last, I was at peace. At that very same moment, Philip telephoned me and said the girl, Teena, and her parents, Susi and George, whom we had visited this morning, had called him, saying they liked Simon very much and would like to proceed with the wedding. I was so excited I couldn't stop praising and thanking the Lord for this amazing news. My brother-in-law told his wife that I was thanking God instead of him since he was doing all the work. He didn't understand that the Lord was using both him and his friend to accomplish His plan and to glorify Himself.

Not a moment was wasted; both families got together on Wednesday, August 30, to finalize the wedding plans. Before anyone left, all agreed that the marriage would take place on September 10 at 11 a.m., which happened to be the same date that had previously been set with the family of the first candidate. Everyone would have to make a tremendous effort for this event to take place in such a short period of time and for it to be as beautiful and perfect as we all hoped it would be.

I feel that it is imperative for me to take this time to thank a very special person. In fact, he's someone whom I had never met before. It is so amazing how God prepares the hearts of men to accomplish His will and His plan. Because George was at the right place at the right time and willing for God to use him, our family was abundantly blessed. He thoughtfully took on the responsibility of reaching out to the priest, reserving the church and the reception hall. It was wonderful to know that the locations were just fifteen minutes away instead of an hour's drive like the first one would have been. He also took even more pressure off our shoulders when he contacted the caterer and the decorator. May the Lord richly bless George and his family, and may He continue to use him in a mighty way.

The church priest was also a great help to us. He had to make many phone calls to find a choir that was available, for there were many weddings taking place that day, and most were already reserved. This kind young priest also persevered until he got us a bishop to conduct the wedding service.

Mere words cannot begin to express my gratitude and thankfulness for all that my sister, Valsamma, and my brother-in-law, Philip, did so selflessly and enthusiastically; it would have been impossible for me to have done it without them. Philip, full of energy, worked nonstop, making arrangements for all the details of the marriage, such as getting the photographer, ordering the invitation cards, and many other chores. Shyba, my student, and her husband, Subichan, worked wholeheartedly along with my sister and her husband; they treated the matter as if it were their own family affair. In the meantime, I made the list and began to invite the guests via telephone since there was no time to reach them with a mailed invitation.

Father Abraham Tharakan was number one on the list. I developed a personal trust and a close relationship with him in a short period of time (although we never met face to face). One evening, I telephoned him, and he said, "I was thinking of you, and I just finished praying for the family." I then told him all the above events that had taken place. "It was like Isaac and Rebecca's marriage," he responded. I agreed with him, for I had been thinking about the same since the day the Lord brought George into our lives as a messenger.

Simon Sr. and Maureen arrived on September 4 as planned, and my husband joined me in inviting the guests. Things were moving along very well; Simon and Teena took premarital counseling together. They spent time getting to know each other and were extremely happy. The wedding took place on September 10, between 11 a.m. and noon. Relatives and friends came from many parts of India and the United States. It was an awesome day, and all the guests enjoyed the ceremony and the feast.

A few days later, my sister asked me, "Did you notice how happy Simon is now?"

I told her, "Yes, they are like lovebirds." What a true blessing! An amazing mercy of God!

God answers everyone's prayers, especially those with "a broken and contrite heart, O God, you will not despise" (Psalm 51:17). God answered not only my prayers and those of my family and friends in America but also those of Teena, who lived only five houses away from my sister. Teena revealed to us that after observing Lent for thirteen consecutive Tuesdays and praying at St. Mary's Cathedral, Manarcad, her parish church, for the Lord to bless her with a beautiful marriage to a God-fearing, loving, caring, honest, and humble husband. She also requested Mother Mary to pray the same prayer to her Son, Jesus.

Teena said that after meeting Simon during the twelfth week of Lent, she felt in her heart that he had all the qualities she had been praying for. On the Monday following the thirteenth Tuesday, they got married!

Recently (after I returned to America), Teena told me that although she is looking forward to going to the United States, she has wisely been using the time to witness to her colleagues and many others while waiting for her visa to be approved. Many have said that they intend to follow in her footsteps after hearing her testimony about God's goodness and mercy in answering her prayers. Before we ended our conversation, she said that, to this very day, she keeps thanking God for the miracles He has done in her life. She revealed to me that she and her mother, Susi, were attending the first service at St. Mary's Cathedral on August 27 at the same time Simon and I were praying in a different building of the same church.

Abba Father, we thank You for Your amazing mercy. Saint Mary, Mother of God, and Saint George, we thank you for praying for us!

CHAPTER 14:

GOD'S AMAZING GRACE

Although we had been earnestly seeking a godly Christian mate for both Simon and Maureen, up to this point, we had not found a good spouse for our daughter. One night in late August, my heart was deeply troubled again. For not only had we been unable to find a suitable mate for my oldest child, but we had not even found so much as a possible candidate. This had been grieving me greatly, especially when Maureen told me that she felt like I had been looking only for Simon and not searching hard enough for her. I had never had such a heartbreaking night in my life. I cried out to the Lord, saying, "Lord, I don't know how to pray or what to say to You, but You know everything. Please, speak to me and give me a good night's sleep."

Sometime during the middle of the night, I fell asleep and woke up by 6 a.m. I searched within myself and pondered, "Did God speak to me?" I realized He hadn't and quickly fell back to sleep. It was during this time that a voice came to me and said, "When you are ready, God will provide." Immediately, my burden was lifted, and I began thanking and praising the Lord. I told my sister about this revelation from God. That very same morning, I telephoned Maureen and told her what God had said to me. She replied, "I am ready, Mom." But I was not sure how ready she was.

I knew why God spoke to me in this way: whenever Maureen was feeling discouraged or sad because she had not found a good husband, though she had been searching for years and had talked with various young men, I never failed to comfort and strengthen her by reminding her that God had been working with her step by step and that He would provide, just as Abraham had told Isaac. After our conversations, without her knowing, I would cry out to the Lord, saying, "Father, You heard what my daughter said, and You know the desires of her heart. Please show us the right person for Your child."

After Maureen arrived in India, several young men responded to the ad we had placed for her. We decided to let three of them see her before September 8; they all claimed to like her. Since it would have been too hectic to manage both Simon's wedding on the tenth and entertain Maureen's guests, we put everything on hold for a few days. During this time, we received several additional calls.

One of those three gentlemen's father wanted his son to marry Maureen. He was rushing to set the date before Simon's wedding. The first time I told him, "If it is God's will, it will work," he agreed. This man continued to put pressure on us and kept calling, but when I told him I would have to pray about it, he responded, "Do what you have to do," and that was the end of his calls.

On the following day of Simon's wedding, Lilly, a widow, telephoned me to find out all about Maureen and our family background. She had been in search of a godly, Christian young woman for her son, Jettin. I also asked questions about her family and their background. She told me her husband had been a businessman who lost everything and died of a heart attack. She said they had to sell their land and huge home in order to pay off the debtors and move to another town where her son was working. Lilly had turned to the Lord during those traumas and had been a very prayerful person ever since. Unlike many people who would have sought psychiatric help or possibly become suicidal. When she stated, "I'm living today only because of Him," I knew this was a woman of God. Oh, what a testimony! This reminded me of the hardships that I had been going through in my own life. In addition, Carolyn had experienced the same situation as this widow, except that her husband didn't die. They divorced, which is more or less the same to me—either way, I would be devastated.

During our conversation, Lilly also told me all about Jettin, who was very godly, hardworking, caring, and abstained from tobacco and alcohol. I loved everything about them both and asked her when they could come to see our daughter. She replied that she would talk it over with Jettin and get back to me.

The following day, Lilly called to tell me that her son had responded, "Why bother? First of all, they live too far. They are Americans—they will look down on us."

When I heard this, I was astonished and tried to convince her that we were not that type, but she couldn't do anything against her son. She commented, "We hear the rumors that in America, everybody has boyfriends and girlfriends from a very young age."

I replied, "We brought up our children in the way of the Indian culture."

As soon as I hung up the phone, I heard a voice telling me, "Humble yourself." I kept this to myself.

A couple of days after Simon's wedding, we resumed working for Maureen. We welcomed a few more gentlemen and their families who had set dates to come to see her. Once they met her, they all liked her; each one wanted us to visit their homes in order to discuss wedding plans. Maureen said that a couple of them seemed nice, so we decided to accept those invitations. But, once again, we had to take a break for Simon to catch his flight back home. We spent that night at the home of my husband's younger sister, who lived in the same town as Lilly.

I thought it might be a good idea to have Lilly and Jettin come over to my sister-in-law's place, being they were hesitant about making the long trip to see Maureen. I called Lilly and made the invitation, but she commented about it being on short notice and too late in the evening; if I had contacted them a day ahead of time, they probably would have come.

The following morning, as Simon Sr., Maureen, Teena, and I traveled back to my sister's place, we stopped at the home of one of the young men Maureen had liked and with whom we had made an appointment. We met both his parents and some relatives, but we didn't have a strong feeling that he would be the best candidate for Maureen, so we left for our destination.

Once we arrived home, Lilly called and said, "Suppose our children like each other; what would be the next step, being you have so little vacation time left?" We only had six days—it was September 14, and Maureen had to leave India on September 20. I told her that we could finalize the engagement, go to America, and come back within three months for the wedding. She replied that she would have to talk with Jettin. She implied that she wasn't pleased with the idea. When I mentioned this conversation to Valsamma and Teena, they advised me not to use that tactic with anyone else, for no one in that area would be willing to wait three months—they could lose out on other opportunities for a better candidate.

The next day, we ended up changing our departure date after Maureen stated, "I am not leaving India until I get married." Her reaction probably came as a result of seeing Simon and Teena enjoying their life together. I did not know what could have been going through her mind, but now I knew that she was definitely ready. I was reminded of what God had told me in late August, "When you are ready, God will provide."

Once I confirmed with the travel agent that airline seats were available on the fifth and the sixth of October for our departure, I let Lilly know that we had extended our vacation and we planned to have the wedding before we left for America. Sure enough, when I gave her the news, she was extremely happy. Because Jettin wasn't working the next day (Sunday, September 17), she made an appointment for the two of them to come to see Maureen.

This lovely lady and her son not only arrived on time for their appointment, but they also went out of their way to stop and pray at St. Mary's Cathedral, where Simon and I had prayed on the day he came from America. In fact, Maureen and I had also been there several times to pray. How awesome—it's absolutely supernatural that before any of us had ever met, and over a short period of time, Teena and her mom, Jettin and his mom, Maureen, Simon, and I had all stopped to pray at this miracle-working church. Every year, millions of pilgrims go there to worship. I thank God that, according to my family's history book, our ancestors took part in building this famous church.

Because Lilly and her son were very punctual, it gave Maureen and Jettin ample time to communicate privately and to get acquainted with each other. After their visit, Maureen said she really enjoyed their time together, and he seemed very nice, but she got confused and simply didn't know if Jettin was the right person for her. She prayed and asked the Lord for the wisdom to make the right choice. She felt that He wanted her to listen to the opinion of the majority of the family before making her final decision.

The next morning, Lilly called and said that she and Jettin both liked Maureen very much because she was humble, sincere, and loving. She asked how we felt about coming to her home for a return visit. Without hesitation, I told her we would see them the following day. Before the day was over, we had to visit one more candidate with whom we had already made an appointment, but we returned home disappointed.

Early the next morning, Valsamma and Teena told Maureen and me they both felt that Jettin was definitely the best candidate of them all. I knew instantly that it had to be God who put that thought in their minds in order to make it a majority opinion.

That very afternoon, Maureen, Simon Sr., Valsamma, Philip, and I made the two-hour trip to see Jettin and his family. He and Maureen had an opportunity for a more in-depth conversation. Afterward, she came out of the room with a smile on her face and said, "He's the one!" We all had a very pleasant visit that evening. Both families decided to have the betrothal that upcoming Sunday, with the wedding on Thursday, September 27. That meant we had very little time, exactly seven days, to accomplish everything.

We returned home joyfully, thanking and praising God for His goodness and for all He had done for us. Although I have great compassion and respect for widows, if God had not commanded me, "Be humble!" after my second telephone conversation with Lilly, I would never have kept making all those phone calls; I know for sure that God was working in both of us to accomplish His plan.

As we reached home, everyone began to work harder and harder, especially Philip, of whom it can truly be said, "He ran his race." As for Maureen, she had her own major task to accomplish, which was to change her denomination from Orthodox faith to Roman Catholic, the groom's faith, within four days so that the betrothal could take place.

Philip was so accommodating, knocking on one Catholic church door after another as he searched for a priest who would be willing and able to meet all of our needs. Of course, God graciously led him to one who was very kind and gentle. Although the young priest was busy, he saw our situation and realized how urgent it was; he went above and beyond, making sure we correctly filled out all of the paperwork that had to be submitted to the hierarchy, as well as counseling Maureen for three consecutive mornings.

While all of this was going on in India, in New York, Father John Thomas was preparing and sending out all of the necessary legal church papers. On top of everything else, he went out of his way to keep a dialogue going with the young Catholic priest in India.

As if it weren't enough, we had all the official matters to take care of. We still had to shop for the fabric we needed to make Maureen's betrothal outfit. Once we found the cloth she liked, it had to be taken to a tailor to be perfectly sewn and properly fitted. Next, we had to shop for all of the accessories to match her dress, such as jewelry, makeup, shoes, and purse. Last but not least, we had to find a beautician to take care of the manicure, pedicure, makeup, and hairstyle. We were so blessed to find a wonderful lady who fit the bill for all of these things. She also came and helped us dress Maureen for the betrothal service and for the wedding itself.

The betrothal took place just as it had been planned, on Sunday, September 23, in our place, Kottayam. We now had three days left to get ready for the wedding: the following morning, we headed back to Jettin's town, Cochin (nearly two hours' travel), for a combined shopping trip for him and Maureen. As is customary in our culture, the bride and the family helped choose the wedding suit and accessories for the groom, and then he, along with his mother's great help, chose a wedding trousseaux and some of the accessories for Maureen. We returned home late in the evening and began inviting the guests by phone.

Tuesday morning, after going by the tailor to drop off the material for Maureen's outfit, we went looking for the saris and the attire needed for Lilly, Valsamma, Teena, me, and a few more accessories for Maureen. The last stop on our way home was another tailor, where we dropped off the items that had been purchased and needed to be sewn and fitted. The owner of this shop later told me that because of Maureen's gentle and sweet character and humble nature, she and her workers had been praying for her to get married from the beginning of September, when they first met her. I am so thankful to all the tailors for their prayers, their sincere dedication to our family, and for getting our needs met in such a short period of time. May the Lord abundantly bless each and every one of them.

Since all of the guests were being invited by phone, we had to continue making calls as soon as we arrived back at the house. We spent the entire day Wednesday picking up everything from the tailors that had been dropped off. That included trying it all on and waiting while any necessary alterations were made. By the time we had dinner that evening and made a few last-minute phone calls, we had approximately two hours left to try and get some much-needed sleep. Alarms for Thursday had been set for 2 a.m., for the beautician was arriving at 2:30 a.m. to begin helping all the ladies, mainly Maureen, fix their hair, apply their makeup, and put on their wedding outfits. The photographer was scheduled to arrive at 7 a.m.

Because we were facing a two-hour drive, arrangements had been made for transportation, and the guests were instructed to come early enough to have breakfast. Shortly afterward, the priest arrived, we all had prayer and blessings, and everyone left for the church.

God was so good to us; none of our labor was in vain. Everything, from start to finish, turned out perfect. We arrived at this huge, nine-hundred-year-old, lovely Basilica on time without any interference from traffic or weather. The wedding ceremony took place as scheduled, from 11:30 a.m. to 12:30 p.m. Hallelujah! Praise the Lord, Maureen is now married to a godly, Christian husband. The Lord wiped away my tears! Oh, how wonderful it is, and what peace it gives us to have such loving, faithful, and God-fearing families around us.

The beauty of it all is that my sister and brother-in-law delighted in doing both weddings and were totally involved. They worked their hearts from start to finish because of their love and concern for me and my children. Even Shyba and Subichan worked right along with Valsamma and Philip, graciously helping with both weddings. As I wrote this, the Holy Spirit took me back to my younger age and reminded me of my father's teachings in Psalm 133. I now realize how worthy and practical they came to be. I quote only one verse, "BEHOLD, how good and how pleasant it is For brethren [siblings] to dwell together in unity!" (Psalm 133:1, NKJV). Yes, indeed, they are more worthy than gold and silver or any precious stones. God is so awesome, and His words are alive and true. This psalm was written about three thousand years ago, and it is still active and powerful.

Just as my sister had been praying, we all left India with joyful hearts. All who heard about these marriages were extremely happy and amazed. When people call me to find out about the details, they say it was a miracle and they have never heard of anything like this, especially the children born and brought up in America. I personally cannot stop talking or thinking about it, and I keep thanking and praising the Lord for opening the floodgates of heaven and showering blessing after blessing upon us.

After returning from India, Carolyn and I resumed writing on the conclusion of this book, chapter 12, "From the Beginning to the End," but on November 8, 2012, as I was getting ready to go to her house to finish the work, God spoke to me and said, "Your children's marriage is the closure of this book." This is why I included Simon and Maureen's weddings as the last chapters of this book. Later, I realized this was to show the world that God still uses prophets and prophetesses to deliver His message, just as He did in the times of old, and He never fails to fulfill His promise. Let me refresh your memory; in my distress, I cried out to the Lord every day at the chapel (my Father's house) in St. Luke's Hospital, New York, and there He heard my cry and sent Norma the prophetess with the message on May 12, 2003, saying, "God the Father told me to tell you, 'I know you are troubled because of your daughter, and I will take care of that,'" and surely, He did. All my praise and thanksgiving to You, my Father!

Today I am experiencing His glorious mercy and grace because I trusted in my Lord Almighty; also the many prayer warriors that prayed for my children.

My dear readers, from my own experience, my sincere advice to you is, in your time of trouble, cry out to the Lord and get into a relationship with God through prayer, studying Scripture, and fasting. Sometimes, it may take years, but He will surely answer your earnest prayers; don't ever doubt, keep complete faith in Him, and patiently wait on the Lord, for His timing is perfect. Seek first the kingdom of God and His righteousness with all your mind, your heart, your soul, and with all your strength, and the Lord will provide all your needs, just as Jesus taught us in Matthew 6:33. Jesus promised us, "Ask, and it will be given to you; seek, and you will find; knock, and it will be opened to you" (Matthew 7:7, NKJV). And Jesus said, "Therefore whoever *hears these sayings of Mine, and does them*, I'll liken him to a wise man who built his house on the rock" (Matthew 7:24, NKJV) (emphasis added by the author).

I cannot stress enough to study the Scriptures—the Word of God—especially the teachings of Jesus Christ. Put them into practice; apply them to your daily life; be a follower of Jesus Christ, a true Christian!

May the grace of God be with all of us.

Much love to you all.

To God be the glory!

ADDENDUM

Although both my children got married two weeks apart in September 2012, they didn't have children for many years despite continued prayers. In September 2017, Simon and Teena moved down from New York to be closer to their elderly parents, who could use some of their help.

January 2018 onward, we began to cry out and pray earnestly to the Lord for the forgiveness of their sins, as well as ours, and petitioned, "Father, do not cut off our generation, please." I also requested the whole church, Norma the prophetess, and the prayer warriors who were on the prayer line every morning to pray for my children to have children. Of course, my younger sister cried out every day for them. Many times, during my prayers, the Holy Spirit reminded me of Naomi, and I would cry out to the Lord and say, "Father, Naomi couldn't have the generation to go on, for her husband and both sons were taken from this world. But You made a way and blessed Naomi with a grandson in her arms. You are a way-making God; nothing is too hard for You, Father." God certainly heard our prayers. Teena conceived in November 2019, gave birth to a normal, healthy boy in the summer of 2020, and named him Joshua! Praise the Lord.

Now, my firstborn, Maureen, up in childbearing age, kept her weight the same or even more. Everyone continued to pray for her. I recall someone saying to me, "Tell her to lose weight." That did not turn me down; in fact, my prayers got more intense, and I trusted in the Lord more than ever. During my daily 3 p.m. prayer time, I would cry out, "Lord God, Your Word says You are the same yesterday, today, and evermore. You gave barren women the children; You blessed ninety-year-old Sarah with a son; Rebecca was barren, You blessed her with two sons after twenty years of married life; Rachel was barren, and You blessed her with two sons; You heard the cry of Hannah, and You blessed her with a son, she kept her promise, and You blessed her with another five more children; Naomi was heartbroken, she couldn't have generation to go on, and You blessed her with a grandson, You're a way-making God! And finally, Elizabeth was barren, and You blessed her and her husband, priest Zachariah, with mighty son John the Baptist in their old age. "Is anything too hard for the LORD?" (Genesis 18:14). None! Abba Father, bless Maureen and her husband, Jettin, to have a normal, healthy, godly child. Please do not cut off Lilly, Jettin, and Maureen's generation. The whole group, as mentioned above, and all my sisters continued praying for my daughter, especially Valsamma, who cried out day and night. Despite all these, I gave Maureen certain Bible verses that fit the situation and advised her to read and meditate on them in the morning and at night, and she was obedient.

Our compassionate God heard our cries and prayers, and Maureen conceived in June 2021. At the first doctor's office visit after six weeks of gestation, the doctor gave a certificate of "70 percent miscarriage and 30 percent survival rate." Maureen was a little concerned and said to me, "I wish it was just the opposite." I comforted her, saying, the Lord made you conceive; He is in control of life and death, not the doctor. As soon as we hung up the phone, I would turn to God the Father and cry out to Him. Then, I contacted my prophetess and Valsamma, my best prayer warriors, and asked them for their earnest prayers for the current situation.

After that, Maureen saw a different GYN doctor. Every time she went for any kind of testing for the baby, starting with chromosome count, it was a constant prayer that the baby be a healthy, normal, and godly child. A few months later, a report came that one kidney was not functioning normally; more prayers went up. The final negative report was that there was fluid collection on the left side of the brain. By the grace of God, Maureen had no ill effect during her nine months of pregnancy, not even morning sickness, and brought forth a normal, healthy baby boy in the winter of 2022 and named him Sebastian, in her late forties. Is anything too hard for God? The Lord heard years and years of our prayers and cries of "not to cut off our generation." Oh, what a blessing from above!

The Lord again blessed Teena and Simon with a baby girl in the spring of 2023 and named her Hannah. The Lord blessed us with three grandchildren in less than three years. We are praying to guide and help us to bring them up in the nurture and admonition of God and make them mighty servants of the Lord Jesus Christ.

I wrote these in detail not only to acknowledge what the Lord has done for my family, but also so there may be others who go through similar or other situations, and I don't want them to be discouraged. Instead, have complete faith in the Lord, which can only be attained through His words, and pray unceasingly using the Scriptures that fit your situation. You, too, will be tremendously blessed!

ABOUT THE AUTHOR

Leela Eapen with her helper, Carolyn May

After graduating as a registered nurse from the J. J. Group of Hospitals in Bombay, India, and working for a few years as a staff nurse in another local hospital, I moved to New York City in 1972. Later, I received a Bachelor of Science degree, majoring in health administration and community health, from St. Joseph's College in Brooklyn, New York. I worked in local hospitals and organizations and held various positions in many departments. Some of my positions included intensive care unit nurse, utilization review nurse (audited the medical records of Medicare recipients), utilization review and discharge planner, quality assurance administrator, and home care coordinating manager. In 1998, I felt honored to receive the Best Nurse Coordinating Manager of the Year award from the Home Care Department at Metropolitan Hospital, New York City.

Unexpectedly, in 1998, an opportunity came; God blessed me to accomplish a long-awaited (twenty-six years) passion. I was able to visit the holy land and was abundantly blessed. Who knew a decade later, I would be utilizing this marvelous holy land experience in writing a book such as this?

I have always been active in my church, taught children's Sunday school for many years, and led the women's league for a few years. I have always tried my best to lead a religious life. By the mid-1990s, I started having a great hunger and thirst for studying the Word of God, but I found it very difficult to understand. Due to my strong desire for the truth of God's Word and to defend my faith, I enrolled in a Bible school in midtown Manhattan in 1999, and eight years later, in 2007, I graduated with an advanced certificate. During these school years, God began to do wonders in my life. He heard my prayers and cries and spoke to me through a prophetess in 2003.

This same year, although I'm not a Catholic, I had a deep desire to attend the celebration of the Beatification of Mother Theresa, for I never heard of such a mighty and humble servant like her who served the Lord during my lifetime. (Of course, I have one more admirer who also served the Lord in my lifetime, and that is Saint Billy Graham.) Mother Theresa served the poorest of the poorest in the slums of Calcutta all her life, and like Jesus, she did not retaliate when her enemy spit on her face! I wanted to honor her, so I began to pray about it; surely, God granted me the desire of my heart. My husband and I were blessed to attend the celebration and the Holy Mass for the Beatification of Mother Theresa by Pope John Paul the Second at St. Peter's Square, Vatican City, Rome.

Since 2003, my relationship with God has continued to grow

ABOUT THE AUTHOR

deeper and more personal, and He has become closer to me. In 2005, He gave me the vision and guidance to write His book, and I must say that God is the Author of this book, not me. He even gave me a helper (a total stranger) to assist in my writing. I am merely a messenger.

I have been retired and reside in Georgia with my husband and family. We have been married for over forty-nine years. Here, I am tremendously blessed to serve the Lord in various prisons in the states of Georgia and Florida, and I have an unending passion for teaching the Word of God. Miraculously, in late 2012, the Lord opened the doors at Phillips Transitional Center, a state prison in Gwinnett County, and enabled my writer and me to hold a weekly Bible class and to pray for the residents who live there. Lately, I have obtained a life coaching certification to serve the following populations: returning citizens (newly released from the prisons) and individuals who are lonely, depressed, or have suicidal ideations. My goal is to offer them prayers, spiritual upliftment through the Word of God, and life coaching sessions to empower their life move forward.

Praise, glory, and honor to You, my God Almighty, for directing my path!

If you feel you're being blessed through this book, then please give the glory and honor to God Almighty because the message is from Him and I'm merely a messenger.

God bless you my friend.